# IN THE PINK

## Support for those suffering from cancer

MAUREEN BENNETT, HELEN LONG AND
PAT MOLLAN

# IN THE PINK

## Support for those suffering from cancer

MAUREEN BENNETT, HELEN LONG AND
PAT MOLLAN

## AMBASSADOR INTERNATIONAL
GREENVILLE SOUTH CAROLINA & BELFAST, NORTHERN IRELAND

www.ambassador-international.com

# In the Pink
## Support for those suffering from cancer

ISBN:   978-1-62020-125-1
eISBN:  978-1-62020-177-0

Printed by Bethel Solutions


**Ambassador International**
Emerald House
427 Wade Hampton Blvd
Greenville, SC 29609, USA
www.ambassador-international.com

**Ambassador Books and Media**
The Mount
2 Woodstock Link
Belfast, BT6 8DD, Northern Ireland, UK
www.ambassadormedia.co.uk


*The colophon is a trademark of Ambassador*

# Contents

# FOREWORD

Perhaps it is in the face of pain, or in the moment of fear, or at a time when one tries to protect others from the looming cloud of inarticulate sorrow; or prehaps it is in the slow night watches when everything is hushed and still save for the relentless churning of one's ungovernable mind; whenever it is, there comes that time when we have no power of ourselves to help ourselves. It is then we need an arm to lean on, an ear to hear and a heart to empathise articulated in accents of love.

Within these pages the finger-posts to such resources are amply to be found. Arising from a heartfelt need in the emptiness of a time of trouble Pat Mollan, Maureen Bennett and Helen Long have gathered and ordered small, approachable treasures inviting the seeker to find a way out of shadow into luminosity. There are no easy answers and no clichéd banalities, just reflections that by their very nature engage not merely the mind but also the heart.

Ps 34.8    *Gustate et videte quoniam suavis est*
              *Dominus: beatus vir qui sperat in eo*
Ps 34.8    *O taste and see how gracious the Lord is:*
              *Blessed is the man who hopes in Him*

The Most Revd A E T Harper, OBE, BA
Former Archbishop of Armagh, Primate of All Ireland and Metropolitan

November 2012

# INTRODUCTION

This little volume has been the joint efforts of Maureen Bennett, Helen Long and Pat Mollan, who were challenged by the husband of a patient with breast cancer. As part of her therapy she was offered Buddhist meditation, or Yoga. When she turned these down and asked for some Christian meditations or reflections she was told that no such material existed! This was their starting point, and they hope that more will develop from this first effort, but they offer this as a labour of love and compassion, with their prayers that this may encourage many to seek Jesus the Healer, and that they might find peace and security in his presence.

# DIAGNOSIS

## DIAGNOSIS

Whoso dwelleth under the defence of the Most High: shall abide under the shadow of the Almighty.

I will say unto the Lord, Thou art my hope, and my strong hold: my God, in him will I trust.

For he shall deliver thee from the snare of the hunter: and from the noisome pestilence.

He shall defend thee under his wings, and thou shalt be safe under his feathers: his faithfulness and truth shall be thy shield and buckler.

Thou shalt not be afraid for any terror by night: nor for the arrow that flieth by day;

For the pestilence that walketh in darkness: nor for the sickness that destroyeth in the noon-day.

A thousand shall fall beside thee, and ten thousand at thy right hand: but it shall not come nigh thee....

....For he shall give his angels charge over thee: to keep thee in all thy ways.

They shall bear thee in their hands: that thou hurt not thy foot against a stone.

Psalm 91

(Book of Common Prayer, 1926)

## LOVING GOD

Loving God, I pray you,
On this daunting day
Of cancer diagnosis—
Take my fears away.

Life seems very fragile
Suddenly today—
Future is uncertain—
Take the fear away.

Let me lean on you, Lord
All along the way:
Give me strength and courage,
And keep my fear at bay.

Doctors say my treatments
Begin without delay—
I must have faith in them, Lord—
Take my fear away.

I trust my life to you, Lord
Every single day:
Come and dwell within me
And chase my fears away!

## PRAYER

Father, you know just how scared I am feeling, following this diagnosis I've just been given. Help me to remember that you are far greater and stronger than both my fear and this cancer. In my weakness, I pray for your strength and sustaining grace, that I may overcome my anxieties. And please also remember my family, who are struggling to come to terms with the situation. Hold us all in the palm of your hand, now and always. In Jesus' name. Amen.

# WE SHALL NOT BE 'MOOVED'

*Psalm 34:4 I sought the LORD, and he answered me; he delivered me from all my fears.*

*Isaiah 35:4 Say to those with fearful hearts, "Be strong, do not fear."*

My greatest fear—and the stuff of many a nightmare—stemmed from a real incident involving Maureen and myself as children. We lived in the Police Station next door to a farm in a small Co Tyrone village. One day two black bull-calves broke into our garden while we were playing there. Ever the animal-lover, I saw this as an opportunity to feed them and 'make friends'. It was to be one of the worst mistakes I ever made, as one of them attacked us and knocked Maureen to the ground. I ran screaming to our mother, who came running out. She was just in time to save Maureen from being trampled and, at the very least, badly injured by the beast.

The story ends with a rather comical twist, as a team of policemen was mobilised to round up the animals, one of whom was quickly returned to its field. The other, however, was not so compliant, and gave the gallant RUC men a real run for their money, at one point getting tangled in the rolls of barbed wire that surrounded the station. (It was during the Troubles in the mid-1950s.) However, my one abiding memory is of one of these men holding on to the animal's tail as it careered around the garden, his heels leaving a pattern of skid-marks to tell the tale!

In the week leading up to the hospital appointment, that was to deliver my stark breast cancer diagnosis, I was involved in an almost repeat performance, this time involving three Friesian heifer calves, who were careering around an adjacent residential area. I had been walking my dog round the local football pitches. There were other dramatis personae, including again a doughty police officer—from the PSNI— who helped to get them off the road, but, as the others left, I offered to help the farmer and his wife herd them back into the field. Another mistake, you might think. Probably, but the farmers didn't refuse, so there we were: three against three. The heifers proved very awkward indeed, and I recall one really terrifying moment when I was face-to-face with one in a nightmarish stand-off, not knowing whether I was going to be charged down and beaten up by this large creature. I can tell you that I prayed very hard just then. And my prayers were answered, for soon after that the three miscreants were safely returned to their rightful place; and I to mine, with no harm done.

As I thought about it then, and in the succeeding months, I wondered if my confrontation with that angry heifer somehow symbolised my encounter a few days later with the shocking news of my life-threatening illness. And that I was going to have to face it down in the same way as I had the dangerous and unpredictable beast. I had to confront my fear in the animal, and then confront a different fear in the cancer. Perhaps the safe outcome of the first gave me hope and strength for the second. God had not forsaken me in one time of need, and He would not leave me in this other. And so I drew strength from this sense of assurance, and subsequently went on to prove that the LORD was with me every step of the way, in the bad times and the good. To Him be the glory.

# A PRAYER

Father God, You know how scared I am of this horrible illness, and what it is capable of doing to my body. Help me to remember that you are much greater than it, and that through Jesus you have overcome all the things that we fear most in life. Help me to hold firmly on to you in this struggle, and to know that you are supporting me every step of the way, and will never let me go. What a wonderful assurance this is. In Jesus' name. AMEN.

# REFUGE

*Be merciful to me, O God, be merciful to me, for in you my soul takes refuge; in the shadow of your wings I will take refuge, until the destroying storms pass by.* Psalm 57:1 (NRSV)

I woke in the middle of the night, normally so quiet and peaceful, but there and round about the wind blew and whistled rattling doors and raising a panic inside me. Despite this the dogs were quiet. Perhaps they felt like I did, the rage of tempest whirling and stirring round the house. I wondered what part of the tide we were on and where the water's edge would reach, and would the roof stay on or intact, for the wind seemed so vicious and unremitting. I had gone to bed without thought of storm, but now the wind was blowing across the water, changing its surface from mere ripples pushing the surface faster and higher, and bringing strong destructive forces with it. I tried to take myself away in my mind to the seashore on a sunny day and imagine that I was watching the waves and trying to see if the seventh wave was really bigger, but I couldn't distract myself from the commotion that was going on outside. I couldn't play with unreality. I was stuck where I was in this middle of the disharmony, being tossed to and fro in my turbulent mind. Fear was close by; rising and falling, reflecting the turmoil outside, and increasing its grip inside. I vainly scraped my inner resources to face my fears and trawled my memory for words to allay them. There I was back in the classroom standing to recite the previous night's homework:

'Blow, blow, thou winter wind.
Thou art not so unkind
As man's ingratitude;
Thy tooth is not so keen,
Because thou art not seen,
Although thy breath be rude.'

(Shakespeare, As You Like It, Act II, Scene vii)

It did make me laugh briefly at myself in nervous recitation, but the fact remained, I was still in the middle of this great and unremitting tempest. I needed a more secure place than my memory of the past, and again the Psalmist came to my aid: *Be merciful to me, O God, be merciful to me, for in you my soul takes refuge; in the shadow of your wings I will take refuge, until the destroying storms pass by.* Psalm 57:1

## PRAYER

Lord of heaven and earth, come close to me now in my fear and turmoil. I am truly in the middle of a destroying tempest and need your loving reassurance. Gather me under the shadow of your wings and keep me safe. Soothe my anxious mind and bring peace to my troubled spirit. Help me to know your constancy and care even though all of the uncertainties crowd my thoughts. Scatter them as the wind blows chaff away, and settle peace in my heart, and to you be all the praise and glory. Amen.

# A WOOLLY ~~TAIL~~ TALE

*"See the Good Shepherd Jesus stands*
*And calls His sheep by name;*
*Gathers the feeble in His arms*
*And feeds each tender lamb."*

Breast cancer is the most prevalent cancer among women and at any given time affects 1,000,000 women worldwide.

For a woman to be told *"I'm sorry, but you have breast cancer"* is one of the most devastating diagnoses imaginable, which brings me back to the psalmist, *'My tears have been my food day and night while men say to me all day long, "Where is your God?"* (Ps 42:3)

You see, God rarely gets our attention when all is going well in our lives but boy do we sit up and take notice when things go pear-shaped! God whispers in our joys and shouts in our pain.

God knows us individually; every hair on our head is numbered. Regardless of our problems and our mistakes, God loves us personally. He knows our name and he knows our needs, and He is prepared to meet the deepest longings of our hearts.

Jesus said that sheep respond only to the voice of their shepherd, who calls them all by name John 10:3.

Our Lord couldn't have chosen a more perfect illustration of His love for us. He is the Good Shepherd who *"calls His sheep by* name" who cares for us, who gathers the feeble and weak and ill in His arms and *"feeds each tender lamb"*.

So, let us, as the psalmist says, *"Put your hope in God, for I will yet praise him, my Saviour and my God."* (Ps 42:11)

God is with you right now as you read this, He is with you in your cancer and He will stay with you through all your treatment and beyond. He will never leave you nor forsake you.

If God loved you enough to send His only Son to die for you, then He loves you enough to see you through whatever illness you may be facing. Don't let your soul be downcast, put your hope in God, He will find you, and carry you on His shoulders to safety.

## A PRAYER

Lord God,
This illness is making me depressed.
I am irritated by its aches and pains.
I get tired of doing nothing.
I worry about the extra work I am causing others.
I worry about myself and my future.
O God,
Speak to me in the quietness about your love for me.
Speak to me about Jesus, about the pain he suffered on Calvary's tree.
Speak to me through the silence and loneliness of this cancer.
Lord God, speak to me.
Amen.

# DANDELIONS

*'Beside the lake, beneath the trees,*
*Fluttering and dancing in the breeze'.*

…words which came to mind as I turned into our lane, and saw an amazing array of bright yellow……………….and I had to ask why Wordsworth wrote of the daffodil and ignored the humble dandelion? Well, I answered myself, perhaps because they don't flutter or dance. They do, however, provide a marvellous splash of late Spring colour to our hedgerows, and gardens. With that bright array before me, I was transported to my youth and the wilderness of garden that was home, where we used to pick the dandelions when they had become the frothy seed head of the dandelion clock. Then we would gently blow across the seeds, one o'clock … two o'clock … three o'clock. It could become any time that you wanted. Thirteen o'clock was my favourite. In real time it didn't exist, but there in the garden it was a certainty, a time when you didn't have to do anything, but could let your imagination roam freely. Today's reminiscences brought me to a poem written by Horace Mann:

Lost, yesterday,
somewhere between
sunrise and sunset,
two golden hours
each set with
sixty diamond minutes.
No reward is offered,
for they are gone forever.

Time takes on a new dimension when we receive a difficult diagnosis. It is then that we want to hear, 'The prognosis is good!' We become obsessed with time and frantically measure it, yet the Jazz musician, Louis Armstrong, put his finger on it when he sang, 'We have all the time in the world'. It is truly a matter of our priorities, and learning to live well all the days of our life, whether they are many or few. Thousands of years ago the Psalmist reminding us of God's loving care for each of us wrote: 'My times are in your hands'. Ps 31:15 (NIV)

## A PRAYER FOR TODAY

A glint of colour, a sunrise or sunset draws my mind to you, O God. Give me grace to live each day with gladness and love, through Jesus Christ our Lord. Amen.

# BRINGING GOOD OUT OF BAD

*O Lord, you have searched me and known me.*
*You know my sitting down and my rising up;*
*You understand my thought afar off...*
*For you formed my inward parts;*
*You covered me in my mother's womb.*
*I will praise you, for I am*
*Fearfully and wonderfully made...*
*...Your eyes saw my substance,*
*Being yet unformed.*
*And in your book they all were written,*
*The days fashioned for me,*
*When as yet there were none of them.*
Psalm 139 (NKJ)

On the day of my cancer diagnosis, when I came home, I sat down and prayed. One of the things I remember asking God for was to let some good come out of my illness. Then I just left it all in His hands. I never imagined that a year later, I would have published a booklet of poems on my illness, and raised £1,200 for two local cancer charities. God is just amazing!

There is a true story about a man called Pra Acharn Chan. Having been diagnosed with leukaemia, he made the decision to devote his remaining time to becoming a Buddhist monk. He could hardly have dreamed that 30 years later, not only would he still be alive, but deeply involved in a most unusual monastery.

Situated in a remote part of Thailand, the monks there dedicate their lives to saving animals, giving sanctuary to a whole variety of injured creatures. Visitors say that it is a place where loving care towards all God's creatures can be seen in action.

This story is a reminder to us that cancer is a life-changing experience; but not necessarily in a negative way. Something horrible can be transformed into an opportunity for good, if we only open ourselves to God's guidance.

## A PRAYER

Father, God, I am in a big battle at present, but I know that you are in it along with me. I pray that you will use any of the things I experience through cancer to benefit others. For your dear name's sake. Amen.

# THE BEGINNING OR THE END?

*'I am the Alpha and the Omega,' says the Lord God, who is, and who was and who is to come, the Almighty.* Revelation 1:8 (RSV)

Cancer is not a death-sentence, although some ill-informed members of the public still tend to think so. You should remember that nowadays many, though not all, cancers, are completely curable. And many others can be so well managed that patients' life-expectancy has been vastly increased, not to mention the improvements to their quality of life. The teams of dedicated doctors, nurses and radiographers are doing all they can to maximise the chances of recovery; and, they have at their disposal an ever more sophisticated armoury of drugs and technology to that end.

When you are first told you have cancer, you will naturally want to focus on whatever treatments you require, and to concentrate on just getting through that process. At that stage, it's hard—maybe impossible for some—to imagine the day when you will be through it all and back to your normal life again. Of course, it takes time to get over the side-effects of the strong, cancer-killing drugs, but there will, for most people, be a time when all the treatment is over, and they are cured or in remission. Perhaps it is only now that you can begin to be truly thankful that all the nasty treatment is in the past, and to draw a line under it. Due to the chemotherapy, I was an absentee from the parish choir for about five months, and being cut off from that important part of my church life was very tough on me. I experienced a sense of disconnection, which was very

23

real and hard to bear. It was wonderful to be able to take up the reins again, in March 2010, and once more to really feel part of the worship and the community again.

## SPRING

There's light at the end of the tunnel,
It comes with the Spring of the year,
I'm through the worst part of my treatment,
And my strength is returning, it's clear.

As Spring is advancing through nature,
My chemo is over and done;
There's a springiness back in my footsteps
For hard times are banished and gone.

Springtime  is a wonderful season,
As it slowly awakens the earth,
A season of hopeful beginnings,
Perennial time of new birth.

For soon we will celebrate Easter
And all that its message proclaims—
As our joy at the end of Lent's darkness
Is kindled to quickening flames.

The blackbirds have started their singing,
Sure sign of the sweetness of Spring—
And I have returned to the choir,
Relieved that I, too, can still sing!!

The light at the end of the tunnel
Is beckoning me to advance,
And as I emerge from the darkness
I feel my feet itching to dance!!

## PRAYER

Father, thank-you, thank-you, thank-you for all that you have done for me over the past months. Thank-you for using the skills of the medical team to restore me to health. I ask you to continue to bless them and the vital work that they do. And use me now, and in the future, to live and work to your praise and glory. In Jesus' name. Amen.

# FEAR

## YOU'RE NOT ALONE

God is Always Present

*When you pass through the waters, I will be with you.*
Isaiah 43:2

Being alone with a frightening problem is very difficult. Isaiah wrote words from God to encourage the people in their most difficult time. He reminded them of their history, of when they fled from Egypt where they had been slaves and were faced with the Red Sea, and no means of getting across. He reminded them of the fact that God parted the waters so that they could pass over before the pursuing armies of the Egyptians could follow them. He also reminded them of the crossing of the River Jordan, when God had again parted the water for them and they could cross safely. God's promise is: 'when you pass through the waters, I will be with you'. It reminds them of very difficult times when they were in danger that God was with them. Sometimes the troubled waters around us seem to overwhelm us, but God's words are sure and true, 'when you pass through the waters, I will be with you'.

His word also says 'when' and not 'if', which means that we will all have difficult times in life, but he also says 'pass through', which tells us that it is not static. There will be change; a beginning and thanks be to God, an end. Our troubled times only last for a time and through them God is with us. His presence is as close to us as breathing; closer than hands or feet. He has promised that he will be there, and he is true to his promises.

## PRAYER

Lord Jesus, may I feel your presence very near to me now. Hold me with your strong arms so that I am not afraid. I know that your word says that you will be with me, and I trust you for that. Help me to concentrate on you and understand that this trouble is only for a while, and that you are with me the whole time. Thank you for your gift of love. Amen.

# CHANGE

God is our Refuge

*God is our refuge and strength, a very present help in trouble.*
*Therefore we will not fear, though the earth should change...*
Psalm 46:1,2a

..though the earth should change. We have all seen the devastation of earthquake changes on TV and the faces of the people stunned and in shock, and realised that things would never be the same again. Yet the Psalmist points us to God in the desperate situation, and assures us that 'we will not fear'. He is looking to God for safety and strength to cope with what is happening round about him, and encouraging others to realise that God alone is our help in times of trouble. If we worship, honour and obey God then he is present with us, a source of strength when the storms surround us, and it seems that the waves are going to sweep over us. His assurance is that even if things happen, that change the perspective of our landscape, we will not fear because God is there for us in our problems and difficulties.

## PRAYER

Lord, my earth appears to be changing round about me and I am afraid. Please take that fear from me, because I know that you, and you alone, are my safety and my strength. Amen.

# THIN ICE OR SOLID ROCK

*He drew me up from the desolate pit, out of the miry bog, and set my feet upon a rock, making my steps secure.*
Psalm 40:2 (NRSV)

It was very cold at 7.30 am, as I left for work to make the twenty mile drive to Belfast. Although the air was cold on my face, I saw no ice on the ground. As I passed along the narrow winding roads between the Clay Lakes I noticed a solitary bird on one lake. It captured my thoughts because it was simply standing there, on the water. I could hardly believe it, so I slowed down and stopped for a closer view. There was this lonely moorhen some distance out from the water's edge standing on the water. As I watched it lifted one leg gingerly, raising its outsized foot slowly, and stepped forward ever so carefully. It then looked round and repeated the slow movement forward. I could have laughed out loud, because there was this bird to all intents walking on the water. It took me a moment to fully comprehend that the lake was frozen over, and that the moorhen was cautiously stepping out on ice. It certainly was well out of its comfort zone. Where it should have been free to swim and move about in the lake, it was confined to a hazardous walk on the icy lake's surface. There is no doubt that it was perplexed, as the conditions were far from normal.

How easily in the course of life we too may be disturbed from our normal existence. Perhaps it was the difficult diagnosis that drew us from our comfort zone, or the uncertainty about treatment and its outcome that removed our equanimity and left us tottering

29

uncertainly, feeling that our feet have left us. How we long for assurance that all will be well, but often none comes and we are left feeling isolated in the uncertainty. We often talk about rock-solid guarantees, but here none come. However the Psalmist points us to God. He writes: *He drew me up from the desolate pit, out of the miry bog, and set my feet upon a rock, making my steps secure.* Psalm 40:2

He also writes: *For God alone my soul waits in silence; from him comes my salvation. He alone is my rock and my salvation, my fortress; I shall never be shaken.* Psalm 62:1,2

## PRAYER

Father, thank you for the unshakable security I have in you. Give me grace to wait on you in silence, and answer my fervent prayer. Slow my anxious thoughts and hide me from fear and uncertainty. Help me to know that I am secure in you and that you will never leave me nor forsake me. Give me an appreciative heart for all who have care of me and my treatment. Touch me with your healing and renew and refresh me that I may be a blessing to all around me, and may your praises always be in my mouth, through Jesus Christ our Lord. Amen.

# THE UNCERTAINTY OF ILLNESS

*'Do not be anxious about anything, but in everything, by prayer and petition with thanksgiving, present your requests to God. And the peace of God, which transcends all understanding, will guard your hearts and your minds in Christ Jesus.'* Philippians 4:8

There are very few things in life that you can be certain of except, as someone said, *'death and taxes'*. Even when we fall ill, things are never usually straightforward and there are many questions to be asked and answered in order to remove the uncertainty that surrounds a cancer diagnosis. Where is the cancer? How big is it? What grade is it? Is surgery an option? Will I need chemotherapy? Will I need radiotherapy? How do I tell my family? Will I lose my hair? Will I lose my life?

I was with my sister at every stage of her diagnosis of and treatment for breast cancer. We knew there was something wrong when we were kept waiting after her initial examination and biopsy. Our fears grew when the Breast Cancer Nurse took us to another room where, she said, the Doctor wanted a word. It was then that we were told Helen had Breast Cancer and that it was Grade Three and aggressive. I thought I had a handle on my emotions but Helen told me later that my face "said it all". I think we both went home in total shock. I know I was thinking, *'This is not happening. It just doesn't make sense. Haven't we been through enough with nursing both our parents through terminal cancer?'* And then, the almost inevitable question, *'Why is God doing this to us, to our family?'*

The God we know, through Jesus Christ, does not willingly afflict his children. There is not one single instance in all the gospel accounts where Jesus told someone that their illness was the will of God. Nor is there even one case where Jesus refused to heal someone by suggesting that illness would strengthen their character.

Sickness is not God's will, and that is something of which you can be certain. If we accept, as some people claim, that '*it is God's will that I am sick*', and if we want to do God's will, then why would we ever consult a doctor, or take medicine, or pray to be healed? Surely that would be going against God's will?

We cannot know and we cannot understand, all the elements involved in the healing process, but we must believe that God's will is for health. There is no uncertainty about that. '*Do not be anxious about anything, but in everything, by prayer and petition with thanksgiving, present your requests to God.*' Our Bible tells us to bring our prayers before God, particularly for those who are sick. Our world is full of tribulation and suffering and uncertainty. God does not promise to remove this suffering from us but he has promised to walk alongside us throughout our earthly pilgrimage; even when we walk through the valley of the shadow of death, we are not to be afraid for God is there with us. There is nothing we will suffer that He has not suffered before us, and in this world of uncertainty, that is something of which you can be certain.

*And the peace of God, which transcends all understanding, will guard your hearts and your minds in Christ Jesus.*'

## PRAYER

Lord, there is so much about my illness that makes me uncertain. I feel that I am travelling along a Via Dolorosa. Grant me that peace, which passes all understanding, the peace that reassures me that I can be certain about your love for me and that you will never cause one of your children a needless tear. Lord, grant me your peace. In your name I pray.    Amen.

## NO FEAR

I will not be afraid

*I keep the LORD always before me; because he is at my right hand, I shall not be moved. Therefore my heart is glad, and my soul rejoices; my body also rests secure.*
Psalm 16:8,9

The writer of this Psalm is making a conscious decision to look to God; because he understands that it is in God's care that he will be safe. He knows that he cannot depend on things round about him, like nice weather or a good meal, or even some of his friends. Underneath his words you can tell that he knows what it feels like to be afraid in life, even of life. Maybe his job had fallen through. Perhaps his heart has been torn by losing the love of someone, and all his future looks bleak. Perhaps he has discovered that he has a severe health problem. These are the hurting experiences of life, and the difficult question is, can he trust God? However, he makes the active choice to seek God. This is how he comes through the loneliness of his distress, because he searches for God. Now, despite his situation he is able to smile again; he can laugh and joke again; all because he got a grip on the conviction that had all but slipped through his fingers; that God cares, and is always at hand, and still has pleasures to give him. This brings him the deep peace of contentment.

## PRAYER

Father I do not know what today will be like, what troubles or joys will come my way. I do not know how well I shall feel, what the test results will be, or what other burdens I shall have to carry. But I know that you care for me and I know that you are with me, and in your presence I feel secure. Amen.

# PER ARDUA AD ASTRA

(Through Adversity to the Stars) RAF Motto

*O Lord, our Lord, how majestic is your name in all the earth!*
*You have set your glory above the heavens.*
*From the lips of children and infants you have ordained praise*
*Because of your enemies, to silence the foe and the avenger.*
*When I consider your heavens, the work of your fingers,*
*The moon and the stars, which you have set in place,*
*What is man that you are mindful of him, the son of*
*man, that you care for him?*
*You made him a little lower than the heavenly beings*
*And crowned him with glory and honour...*
*...O Lord, our Lord, how majestic is your name in all the earth!*
Psalm 8 (NIV)


## DARK NIGHT OF THE SOUL

Night.
Black, dark night;
And sleep a distant aspiration...
Night.
Black, dark thoughts,
Scuttle through my brain
Like an army of busy, gnawing mice.
What is the future for me?
Is there a future for me?
Panic, a cold, blind sweat...

Get up out of bed:
Maybe a cup of tea will help,
Even if it tastes yuck,
Thanks to the chemo…
While the kettle boils
Open the back door, step out into the black world;
Gaze at the blind, black sky…

Out there, behold, the stars are out,
Their pricks of light
Piercing the velvet blackness—
And there is the moon, almost full—
And I recognise the planet Jupiter just a little
Further south, at the same elevation—
And see—
The Plough—
And Orion—
What wonders of creation
Are peppering the heavens up there—
Not at random, but every one in its ordained place
In the firmament,
Held there by the creating Will and Word of God…

Just as I am held
Very tenderly by his steadfast love
As I pass through this viscous vale of misery:
'I will never leave you, nor forsake you.'
This is a promise to hold on to;
After all,
'Darkness and light to thee are both alike.'

## PRAYER

Loving Father, help me through this night, and all the other nights that lie ahead, when sleep eludes me; or when I wake up in the lonely early hours, with that awful feeling of dread. Help me to remember that your Son, Jesus, experienced similar feelings in the Garden of Gethsemane, on my behalf. And that he has ultimately overcome those two monsters, fear and death. Let the light of your love and mercy shine into my heart and soul, to banish any darkness that remains there. Amen.

# WILDERNESS

## THE VALE OF TEARS

"Woman," he said, "why are you crying? Who is it you are looking for?"
John 20:15

When we are given a devastating diagnosis regarding our health, many, many questions will flood our mind and many accusations also. *"Why me God?"* No matter how exciting our Christian walk may be or may have been in the past, most of us come to those difficult times when we do not know which way to turn. Such feelings of inadequacy sweep over us like a dark shadow which seems to reach into the very depths of our being and we ask the question, *"Where is God in all of this?"*

Things can go horribly wrong even when we are doing everything we can to live a good life. You don't have to be living in deliberate sin and shaking your fist at God for something to go wrong. The harsh reality is that bad things do happen to good people.

So, WHERE IS GOD when we need him most? Well, he is right where he said he would be, just as he was with Mary Magdalene in her sorrow in the Garden of Gethsemane, he is right in the middle of our tragedies. He is never absent from our problems and our troubles and our sickness. He is right there ready and waiting to help us to handle them.

The Bible tells us that Christ has promised he will never leave us or forsake us (Hebrews 13:5). God is with us in the midst of our sorrows. The prophet Isaiah says, *"In all their affliction, he was afflicted."* God does share in our suffering.

Our problem is sometimes the same as that of Mary Magdalene; she did not recognize Christ, even though he was standing right beside her! Why? Remember what Jesus said to her (and I much prefer the King James version of Jesus' words to Mary) – "Woman, why weepest thou, whom seekest thou?" Did Mary not recognize her Lord because she couldn't see through her tears or was it because she couldn't draw her eyes away from the empty tomb?

This is all too often our problem also. We are concentrating so hard on whatever it is that is troubling us; we are giving it our 100% attention to the exclusion of everything and everyone else. We are so engrossed in our own problems and troubles, our eyes are so full of tears for ourselves that we fail to see who is walking alongside us. Like Mary Magdalene, we have turned our backs on Jesus to concentrate on ourselves.

Let us turn back and face Christ who is there to help us to carry our burdens, our illness, our worries and anxieties. Let us lay them all at the foot of the cross and when he calls our name, let us turn around and cry out, *"Rabboni!"*

I come to the garden alone
While the dew is still on the roses
And the voice I hear falling on my ear
The Son of God discloses.

And He walks with me, and He talks with me,
And He tells me I am His own;
And the joy we share as we tarry there,
None other has ever known.

He speaks, and the sound of His voice,
Is so sweet the birds hush their singing,
And the melody that He gave to me
Within my heart is ringing.

I'd stay in the garden with Him
Though the night around me be falling,
But He bids me go; through the voice of woe
His voice to me is calling.
*Charles Austin Miles*

A garden in Jerusalem today near the Garden Tomb

# THE WAITING GAME

*The LORD is good to those whose hope is in him, to the one who
seeks him; it is good to wait quietly for the salvation of the LORD.*
Lam 3:25,26 (NIV)

Have your reached rock bottom? Do you feel alone? Sometimes
that is just where we need to be, because then, the only way is up! It
is then that we turn to God and really seek him with all our might.
We seek him as our close companion in the darkness, and he comes
bringing us renewed hope.

It was the hours that Elijah had spent in prayer with God that
brought fire from the sky to ignite the sacrifice on the altar when
he challenged the prophets of Baal on Mount Carmel. (1 Kings
18:16ff) It was this demonstration that convinced King Ahab that
the Lord was indeed God.

When God called Jonah to speak to the people of Nineveh
he ran away, and ended up swallowed by a whale. It was there in
the darkness of the belly of the whale that he was forced to turn
back to God and connect with him. (Jonah 1:17ff) This was what
prepared him to urge the Ninevites to repent of their sins and turn
again to God.

It was because Shadrach, Meshach and Abednego refused to
bow down to king Nebuchadnezzar, and prayed only to God that
the king had them thrown into the fiery furnace. However, God
protected them and they were not harmed by the flames. This was

a mighty sign to king Nebuchadnezzar. (Daniel 3:14ff) Nor did the lions harm Daniel when Nebuchadnezzar threw him into the lions' den. (Daniel 6:16) He was kept safe. God shut the mouths of the lions as Daniel had trusted in him.

It is good to be reminded of these heroes of faith, and to learn that they spent time in prayer with God. May their example bring encouragement to you when it is needed.

## A PRAYER FOR TODAY

Dear Lord, I find waiting very difficult. I think I have begun to realise that you wait. You have waited so long for me to come to you. I am impatient and I want to know you better, but I know that it takes time and I need to spend more time with you. Help me to make that space into which you can speak, and please Lord, speak loudly to me, that I may really hear you, and know what you want for me. Give me strength and courage to do whatever you ask, for I ask in Jesus name. Amen.

# WORRY? WHO NEEDS IT?

*'Do not be anxious about anything, but in everything, by prayer and petition, with thanksgiving, present your requests to God. And the peace of God, which transcends all understanding, will guard your hearts and your minds in Christ Jesus.'*
Philippians 3: 6–7

For several years a woman had been having great trouble sleeping because she was worried about her house being burgled. One night, her husband heard a noise and went downstairs to investigate. When he got there, he actually did come upon a burglar. *'Good evening'*, he said, *'I'm delighted to see you. You must come upstairs and meet my wife. She has been expecting you for the last ten years.'*

The word WORRY comes from an Anglo-Saxon word which means TO CHOKE so, when we worry, we are actually choking ourselves. Now WORRY may not be a disease in itself but it causes much DIS-EASE.

Worry is a mild form of atheism, living as if God either doesn't exist, doesn't have any power, or can't be bothered using his power on our behalf. You see, our lives are like the underside of a tapestry, or a piece of knitting where we can see all the joins, the knots, very messy but very necessary. God, the Master Weaver is creating a beautiful pattern, but right now, in our pain, our illness, we can't see that pattern on the right side, we can only see the underside, full of knots and loose ends and joins.

*'Do not be anxious about anything'.*

Count your blessings, name them one by one. During times of trouble, we should try to dwell on good things. Think about God's blessings – his provision and his care. If we have a physical problem, let us try to focus on the thousands of bits of our bodies that are in perfect working order. Most importantly, as Paul said to the Christians in Philippi, we should cast all our worries and anxieties on God. He can deal with them much better than we can. Let us hand them all over to God and let him do the worrying. We can trust God to be there, to care for us, to provide for us: In the words of Joseph Scriven who was no stranger to tragedy:

'What a friend we have in Jesus,
all our sins and griefs to bear!
What a privilege to carry
Everything to God in prayer!
O what peace we often forfeit,
O what needless pain we bear,
All because we do not carry
Everything to God in prayer!'

If our worries aren't worth praying about, they aren't worth worrying about.

Just imagine God sending us an office memo in which he says,

Christian, today I will be handling all of your problems. Please remember that I do not need your help. Kindly put all your worries in the SFJTD (something for Jesus to do) box. It will be addressed in my time, not yours. Once the matter is placed into the box, do NOT hold onto it or remove it. Holding on or removal will delay the resolution of your problem. Because I do not sleep nor do I slumber, there is no need for YOU to lose any sleep. Rest my child. If you need to contact me, I am only a prayer away.

## A MORNING PRAYER

Father, help me to realise that there is nothing going to happen to me today that together you and I can't handle.
Amen.

# THE PRIVILEGES OF TRIAL

*"I consider the sufferings of this present time are not worth comparing with the glory about to be revealed to us"*
Romans 8: 18-25

I know of no one who is immune to suffering and disappointment. All of us have bad things happen to us. The apostle Paul is a shining example of the Christian response to disappointment, pain and suffering. In the midst of his suffering, Paul took certain comfort in knowing that Jesus had walked that road before and was not going to abandon him. And when things got really bad, when Paul was in prison and all his friends and supporters were being hunted down and persecuted, what did he say? *"I consider the sufferings of this present time are not worth comparing with the glory about to be revealed to us."*

We can hear a real echo of Paul's misery when he says, *"Our outer nature is wasting away."* He means that his body is wasting away and the word for "wasting away" is used for rust eating through iron, of moths eating through cloth, of starvation emaciating the body.

Sometimes it is good to liken ourselves to a bar of iron which, standing alone, is worth about £1. When wrought into horseshoes, it is worth £2. If made into needles, it is worth about £70. If it is made into cutting blades, it is worth £650. If it is made into springs for watches, it is worth £50,000. What a drilling the poor bar must undergo to be worth this! But the more it is manipulated, the more it is hammered and passed through fire, and is beaten and pounded and polished, the greater its value.

Those who suffer most are capable of yielding most. So, we stand in the midst of our pain and look to God with hope in our hearts. With hope we can look at our present situation and see, not only what is, but also what is yet to come. The hopeful Christian is like a farmer who looks at a freshly tilled and planted field and can see the harvest that is ahead.

Whatever problems you are facing today, know that your loving Father in heaven has a plan to redeem your life and bring you into His glory. Bear your burdens in hope and confidence and keep Paul's words close to your heart

## A PRAYER

Father, I know that the sufferings of this present time are not worth comparing with the glory about to be revealed to us. Help me to hold onto this knowledge as I pass through this difficult time. Forgive my human weakness and help me to trust in your promises. When I cannot express my deepest longings and hopes in words may your Holy Spirit intercede with sighs too deep for words, through Jesus Christ our Lord. Amen.

# QUIS SEPARABIT?

Romans 8:

*I consider that the sufferings of this present time are not worth comparing with the glory that is to be revealed to us...*(v18)

*We know that in everything God works for good with those who love him, who are called according to his purpose...*(v28)

*If God is with us, who is against us? He who did not spare his own Son but gave him up for us all...*(v31b-32a)

*Who shall separate us from the love of Christ? Shall tribulation, or distress, or persecution, or famine, or nakedness, or peril, or sword?...* (v35)

*I am sure that neither death, nor life, nor angels, nor principalities, nor things present, nor things to come, nor powers, nor height, nor depth, nor anything else in all creation, will be able to separate us from the love of God in Christ Jesus our Lord.* (v38,39)

(RSV)

What a wonderful guarantee this is. While we are travelling along this difficult and dangerous road, we need to hold these words close to our hearts, and really believe in them and their power to help us, and see us through. Saint Paul, the author, suffered many tribulations as he travelled to proclaim the Gospel, yet he is emphatic here about the love of God surrounding us, wherever we go, whatever happens. It transcends everything, no matter how bad the going gets.

During my chemotherapy treatment, there were a few times

when I felt quite down; not specifically because of my illness, but probably because I was more emotionally fragile at that time. However, I found that God always sent somebody to rescue me from those 'tearful times'. In his love, he knew where my need was, and with perfect timing he gave me the succour I craved, often from an unlikely and unexpected source. He has miraculous ways of healing our small miseries as well as our much larger ones.

## A PRAYER FOR TODAY

Father God, help me to remember that you are in control of my whole life; that you know when my need is greatest, and will respond to that need in your own amazing way. Even when I feel unable to pray, let me feel your loving presence with me, giving me reassurance, comfort and peace. In Jesus' name. Amen.

# TRIALS AND STREAMS IN THE DESERT

One of the most moving experiences I have ever had was that of a Eucharist Service in the Judean Wilderness during a Pilgrimage to the Holy Land. We had a bit of a climb slipping and sliding on the dry earth to get to a flat piece of ground. The Dead Sea was just out of sight and we could see the Biblical mountains of Moab (now Jordan) in the background.

Dotted across the landscape were the black tents of the Bedouins and incongruously perched above nearly every one of them was a satellite dish!

The Bedouins and their camels stood close by as we celebrated the Eucharist, but didn't approach us with their wares until the service was over.

It is a very eerie and humbling experience to stand in the middle of a wilderness and imagine Jesus' spending forty days and forty nights there, being tempted by the Devil.

The desert is a harsh and inhospitable wasteland, a place devoid of people, animals and vegetation. The daytime heat can kill as can the cold at night. It is a place stripped of the essentials of life, but perhaps it is because of this barrenness that we can see things more clearly. And so it is with the deserts in our lives, those times when we are suffering from illness or bereavement or abandonment or betrayal. It is in the desert that we are forced to see things as they really are, no distractions, no disguises. We are forced to face our essential helplessness, our loneliness, our brokenness. There is nowhere to hide. The desert is a very human place to be.

But, with all its loneliness and desolation, the desert has been the backdrop of the most significant encounters between God and His people. There Hagar and Ishmael found deliverance, Moses encountered the burning bush, and the Israelites, escaping from Egypt were miraculously sustained by the manna from Heaven. Elijah found refuge in the desert and hope in his despair and, as mentioned earlier, our Lord faced fierce temptation, found strength to resist and a renewed understanding of his relationship with his Father. Yes, the desert experience has become one of the most significant images of the life of faith.

Brother Roger of Taize wrote: *'When desertions, doubts, discouragements and the silences of God seem to cover everything, will you discern the desert flower?......*

*Didn't you know? In the desert of the heart there were unfailing resources welling up, a life within, an inner light.'*

It is just at the point where we are about to faint, when we cry out in despair, *'My God, my God, why have you forsaken me?* (Matthew 27:46), that God speaks to us and his grace confronts us. Amazingly, we will discover that life-spring, that hidden well where God is present and we might even catch a glimpse of a beautiful desert flower. The peace that God gives us is not a freedom from the storms of life, but a unique strength and comfort amid those storms. He will come alongside us and take us by the hand to lead us through the desert of illness or grief or pain.

God is to be found in every desert.
*See the streams of living waters,*
*Springing from eternal love,*
*Well supply thy sons and daughters,*
*And all fear of want remove,*
*Who can faint while such a river*
*Ever flows their thirst to assuage:*
*Grace which, like the Lord the giver,*
*Never fails from age to age.*

*John Newton based on Psalm 87:2 and Psalm 46:4*

## "O LAMB OF GOD, I COME!"

*'Him that cometh to me I will in no wise cast out.'*
John 6: 37  (KJV)

What Jesus is not saying here is that we have to wait until we think we are good enough and worthy enough to come to him. Friends, we would be waiting a very long time because we will never be "good" enough.  Do you remember Mrs. Alexander's words in her beautiful hymn "There is a green hill"?  She wrote,

'There was no other good enough
To pay the price of sin.
He only could unlock the gate
Of heaven and let us in.'

We are to come to Christ, just as we are, with our heavy burdens of whatever description.  He knows our worries, our fears, our dilemmas and He invites us to come 'just as we are' and He will do the rest.  Another hymn writer, Charlotte Eliott, for whom a severe illness left her almost a complete invalid for most of her life wrote,

'Just as I am, thou wilt receive,
Wilt welcome, pardon, cleanse, relieve;
Because thy promise I believe,
O Lamb of God I come.'

Whatever our desert experience or whatever our burden is, be it illness, bereavement, family problems, it usually involves a sense

54

of feeling utterly alone, an inner isolation, but Jesus assures us that He has been there also. The best, the only way to approach the merciful throne of God's grace revealed in Christ is, **'Just as I am'**.

'Just as I am, poor, wretched, blind;
Sight, riches, healing of the mind,
Yea, all I need in Thee to find,
O Lamb of God, I come.

## PRAYER

O Lamb of God,
to whom we come for healing and relief,
break down the barriers of sin and division
that wound your world.
Give to all your people the comfort of your grace
and the power of your Spirit
to convince us
of the breadth, length, height and depth
of your everlasting love.

Amen.

# DON'T YOU CARE GOD?

*"Who then is this, that even the wind and the sea obey him?"*
Mark 4:41 (NRSV)

It might seem strange to some people to find Jesus in the middle of a crisis. We are more inclined to look for him in some quiet harbour, far removed from howling winds and roaring waves, but Jesus is right at home in the midst of chaos. He was born in a stable; he grew up in a village with a poor reputation; he spent much of his time with people who were mentally, physically and morally sick. He died a cruel, ugly death, surrounded by a mocking, murderous crowd.

You and I will never encounter any frightening experience that is unfamiliar to Him. He has seen it all right down to the edge of that black hole, where God himself seems to have forsaken us. No trouble will ever touch us until it has been filtered through the heart of God.

Jesus knows all about storms both literally and metaphorically. That is one of the reasons why we can trust Him, because He has been there before and He will be there again but this time it will be with us. Jesus cares.

Many times in our lives, perhaps at this very moment, storms toss us around like tiny corks on the ocean of life. The gusting winds of worries about the past and the angry waters of anxieties about the future, can scare us out of our wits. At other times, a state of blackness can be frightening, like a thick blanket thrown over you, where suddenly all is dark and you feel as if you are suffocating. At such times, when we feel as if we are at the bottom of a pit, Jesus appeals to us to trust in his mighty power. It is at the point where we are about to faint, that God gives us the strength to go on. So we must never doubt in the darkness what God has promised in the light.

Apparently, the eagle is the only bird which renews its strength by renewing its wings. As it gets older, its wings begin to make a noise and its beak grows callouses, which means that it is less able to catch its prey. So it goes to some secure place and plucks out all of its feathers and rubs the growth off its beak. New feathers grow. We need to go through a similar process; to shed our feathers of self-reliance, to let go of what we have so far relied on to survive and let God give us His feathers.

When we pass through the storms of life, let us keep our focus fixed, not on the storm, but on God. Let us never doubt in the darkness what God has promised in the light. Within His encircling power we always stand, and on every side we feel His hand.

## PRAYER

Lord, when we cry out to you, "Don't you care if we drown"? quieten our hearts by your words, "Peace, be still". You give us that peace that the world cannot give. Don't ever let us doubt in our darkest hour, what you have promised us in the light. May your peace which passes all understanding, keep our hearts and minds in Christ Jesus in whose name we pray. Amen.

# SWALLOWS

It's bin day, and that may be no problem for you, but if like me, you live at the end of a long farm lane, and you forgot to leave the bin by the road side last night, then there's some quick work to be done. It's not a mindless task, for the round trip is over half a mile, and there's plenty of interest on the way. Frequently above me on the telephone wire are swallows. How grateful I am for the natural surrounding pasture where cattle still graze, and there are sufficient insects to attract these summer visitors, that nest in our neighbouring outbuildings. It is hard to imagine that these little birds migrate from Africa, south of the Sahara, a distance up to 6000 miles. Sad to think that the continuing spread of the Sahara Desert may be making this formidable barrier increasingly difficult for swallows to cross. There are also changes in farming practice throughout Europe which may be reducing the number of nest sites and flying insects.

The Psalmist was aware of these birds for he said: *Even the sparrow finds a home, and the swallow a nest for herself, where she may lay her young, at your altars, O LORD of hosts, my King and my God.* (Psalm 84:3)

It's not just our swallows that are in decline, so also are sparrows. But Jesus said:

*Are not five sparrows sold for two pennies? Yet not one of them is forgotten in God's sight. But even the hairs of your head are all counted. Do not be afraid; you are of more value than many sparrows.* (Luke 12:6,7)

## A PRAYER FOR TODAY

Dear Father God, I am now more aware of my hair than I have ever been. It is comforting to understand that you know all about me, even down to the number of hairs I have on my head. Remind me of this when I feel self pitying and of little worth; and put a song in my heart, for Jesus sake. Amen.

# UNCERTAINTY

## WAITING PATIENTLY
Learn to Wait Patiently

*I waited patiently for the LORD; he inclined to me and heard my cry. He drew me up from the desolate pit, out of the miry bog, and set my feet upon a rock, making my steps secure.* Psalm 40:1,2

We had very tall hedges of Cypress trees round our garden, which had become so tall that they were keeping the light out. They had to be cut down to size and it was a major task, but now they are looking somewhat sparse. I know that I have to wait patiently for the new growth and fresh green shoots. I must wait. There is no other way. It is so hard to be patient, especially when things are difficult. The Psalmist was somehow stuck in a bad place, which was desolate and depressing for him. Perhaps you feel that today you are in a difficult and lonely place. Our writer cried out to God to set him free. He was desperate, but even in that awful place he waited patiently for the Lord. His wait was not in vain. It is never useless to wait on God. We need also to ask him to give us all the patience that we need and things will happen in due time. I know that my hedge will green over again, and the Psalmist was lifted out of the pit and has his feet set on the rock. He felt secure again. When we wait for the Lord, he will lift our spirits and keep us safe and secure.

## PRAYER

Dear Jesus, this disease is frightening and I feel alone even though my family and friends are round about me. I cannot tell them of the fear or loneliness, but I am telling you, because I know that you understand. You were alone before Pilate and before the High Priests, so you understand being in a bad place. I also know that you did it for me and so I am understood. Thank you. Amen

# DOWN AT THE DUMP

Psalm 8:1, 4, 5 *O Lord our Sovereign, how majestic is your name in all the earth! What are human beings that you are mindful of them, mortals that you care for them? Yet you have made them a little lower than God, and crowned them with glory and honour.* (NRSV)

Recycling for a better present and future; words which were going round and round in my brain. Yes, I believe in recycling, but it is the effort involved in taking all the collected and sorted debris to the recycle point. I don't mind collecting it, or sorting it, but it is taking the cans and glass, and old clothes to the salvage collection that is the bother. Usually I do it when the amount I have gathered becomes significant, but I do it with little grace, and some complaining.

Today, as I reached the reclamation unit, to my added irritation, there was a learner driver in front of me having difficulty with the speed ramps. I simply wanted to empty the car and get it over and done with, but I was forced into a situation of restraint as I felt I shouldn't pass a novice in a tight place. As I waited at the entrance I was surprised by the appearance of a grey wagtail on the top rung of the gate, surveying the surroundings. My impatience disappeared and I watched in delight. It had been some time since I'd seen one of these lovely birds, as I usually see only the pied variety of wagtails in the garden. I wondered, why on earth did they call it a grey wagtail, because it is much more colourful than its name would suggest? Its lemony yellow breast and underneath was quite striking as it wagged its black and white tail, while it surveyed the area. Again I thought, 'Why, little bird, do you come down into the dump; what are you looking for here?' When I returned home I consulted the bird book, to find that grey wagtails were found mostly in England, Scotland and Wales, located by fast flowing rivers or streams, and that they fed on flies and insects. Well that explained it. There was a river close by, and I guess that there would be good insects and flies congregating round the refuse, but according to the distribution map I would not have expected to see him here. It was a very fortunate encounter.

One little yellow breasted bird appeared and my attitude changed completely. The whole day took on a different meaning and I was so glad that I had seen him. From being grouchy and down in the dumps, that little grey wagtail changed my whole outlook and my spirit soared. Unaware of the link I began to sing: '*All things bright and beautiful, all creatures great and small, all things wise and wonderful, the Lord God made them all.*' *(Cecil Frances Alexander 1818-95)* That little bird in all its glory pointed me to its Creator, and my song extolled his glory. As I thought over this I realised again God's great love for his creation and for each one of us. The Psalmist asked: *What are human beings that you are mindful of them, mortals that you care for them? Yet you have made them a little lower than God, and crowned them with glory and honour.* Psalm 8: 4, 5

# PRAYER

Loving God and Father, thank you for the wonder of your creation. Thank you for all the beauty that I see around me every day, even in unexpected places, and help me to look for it everywhere and in everyone. As I notice these things help me to be more appreciative of your goodness and for your care for me. Encourage me to lean on you, knowing that you understand me and want my healing and my peace. Give me grace when I have to wait for attention, and give me a grateful heart for all the people and things that help me and point me to you. I ask in Jesus' name. Amen.

# IT'S ALL GREEK

*"I am the Alpha and the Omega," says the Lord God, "who is, and who was, and who is to come, the Almighty."* Revelation 1:8 (NIV)

Perhaps you haven't studied Greek, but you will probably know that alpha is the first and omega the last letter of the Greek alphabet. When Jesus says that he is the alpha and the omega, he is saying that he is the beginning and the ending; the first and the last, and, in a real sense, he is everything in between. What he starts he finishes! The fact that he finishes what he starts gets my conscience, as I have started many projects with enthusiasm, and they remain in the first stages: the bags of part-knitted garments; the flower bed half dug out; the new cook book bought with the intention of healthier eating, but not used. I have a record of tripping when just off the starting blocks. Perhaps that is what makes me give up when I think on spiritual things; even now that I know it matters. Past experience of not completing the task doesn't encourage me to move forward. I have to grasp the truth, that when God starts it, he continues it and he brings it to completion. He calls us to faith in Jesus Christ and, as we turn to him, he develops our Christian character. He has promised that he will never leave us or forsake us (Deut 31:6, 8; Joshua 1:5; Hebrews 13:5), which is very encouraging, particularly when we are scared. We may not always feel that he is with us, especially when we are in the middle of difficult times, and worry and anxiety get the better of us. However, when we are able to leave our apprehensions to one side, we can return to God's promises, and as we hold onto them, they become a reality, and peace returns.

Whatever tight corner we are in; whatever situation of no escape that confronts us, we need to turn to God and cling to him. It is the most practical and direct approach in the circumstances; to take God at his word. Our Christian experience today is only the beginning. Christ is the living word and he hasn't written us off. He wants to spell out in our lives the complete alphabet of his blessings, from A to Z; from alpha to omega.

All the treasures of God's nature are hidden in Jesus Christ (Col 2:3). We find them written in the words of Scripture. Jesus is the divine alphabet which unlocks the revelation of God. The more we allow him to work in us, the more we receive his treasures of grace.

## A PRAYER TO USE

Lord, I find it hard to know where to begin, and what words to use to express how I feel, but you are the alphabet of life; the shaper of words and actions; the beginning and end of all things. I am very vulnerable at the moment and need my family and friends to understand that I just want peace. Give them and me your special grace for this moment, that we may remember that real strength lies in quietness, and trust. I ask in your precious name, Jesus Christ our Lord. Amen.

# SOUL REST

Perhaps at this very minute, you are waiting anxiously for results of a test, as though everything depends on the outcome. For some these results will make you feel that you are on the highest mountain peak, but for others it will be the deepest valley. Indeed, there are times for all of us when 'the only way is up'...when life itself seems a valley experience with no redeeming peaks or vistas, and when no light at all appears to penetrate the gloom of the present moment.

Regardless of the difficulty of dealing with your difficult situation, life does not stop, and there is no point in 'counting the empties' – that is – majoring on the things we cannot do, rather than emphasising the things we can do. When you ask any person who has been successful in life if they have ever failed anything, they will inevitably admit that they have. Many will tell you that it was the turning point, a time of opportunity for them.

Remember that the voice of God is never silent. In every circumstance and situation God is speaking. But are we able to hear and to receive what he is offering? The prophet Jeremiah spoke the words of the Lord saying: *Stand at the crossroads, and look, and ask for the ancient paths, where the good way lies; and walk in it, and find rest for your souls.* (Jer 6:16 NIV) When Jesus is present all is well, and nothing seems difficult; but when Jesus is absent everything seems hard. Whatever the result , may we all say like the Psalmist: *I trust in you, O LORD; I say, "You are my God."*
*My times are in your hand.* Psalm 31:14,15

## A PRAYER FOR TODAY

Dear Lord, I know that you say you are the way and the truth and the life. I do want to walk in your ways, and find the peace and rest that you promise. Take any fear away from me and give me a real sense of your presence with me. I ask in your name, Jesus. Amen.

# TREATMENT

## HOSPITAL

*I will lift up mine eyes unto the hills: from whence cometh
my help?*
*My help cometh even from the Lord: who hath made
heaven and earth.*
*He will not suffer thy foot to be moved: and he that keepeth
thee will not sleep.*
*Behold, he that keepeth Israel*
*Shall neither slumber nor sleep.*
*The Lord himself is thy keeper: the Lord is thy defence upon
thy right hand;*
*So that the sun shall not smite thee by day: neither the
moon by night.*
*The Lord shall preserve thee from all evil: yea, it is even he
that shall keep thy soul.*
*The Lord shall preserve thy going out, and thy coming in:
from this time forth for evermore.*
Psalm 121
(Book of Common Prayer, 1926.)

## HOSPITAL HOSTILITY
God, how I hate hospitals—
Always have—
Hate and fear them—
Especially this one—

With all its cancer connotations.
This is what makes cancer real....
Walking in through these doors
You are entering a
Cancer environment....
A world of fear....
Of negativity...

Well, not, actually.
There is a strange air
Of vibrancy,
And even positivity
About this place....
The doctors and nurses are all so kind, gentle
And understanding.
They have tailored my chemotherapy drugs
Exactly for me;
And later,
The radiotherapy is measured and delivered with
Pinpoint precision.

One lovely lady-doctor tells me
She believes a positive attitude
Really does make a difference—
And I am positive—

And now I find I am able to enter and leave
This hospital
With a confidence
I never thought I had,
In the knowledge that all those treating me
Are God's healing hands
In today's hurting world.

## PRAYER

Father, thank-you for all your wonderful works of healing that are taking place, day and night, in our hospitals. Bless, guide and inspire all doctors, nurses and radiographers, as they go about their routine tasks of healing and helping the sick and suffering.

In Jesus' name. Amen.

# CHEMOTHERAPY.COM

*And he withdrew from them about a stone's throw, and knelt down and prayed, "Father, if thou art willing, remove this cup from me; nevertheless not my will, but thine, be done." And there appeared to him an angel from heaven, strengthening him.* Luke 22: 41-42

19th October 2009
Good morning friends

I got my second blast of chemo on Thursday at 3.30 pm. It really is a whole-day affair. My appointment time was 8.20 am, so you will see what I mean! They have to test your blood, which takes at least an hour.

I am pleased to relate that I had no sickness this 2nd time, because they had cunningly fitted me up with a Syringe Driver. For the uninitiated, this is a little device (worth about £1,000) connected to my tummy by a nurse, and it injects regular doses of anti-emetic into my system. You end up having to carry it around with you over your shoulder, and it tends to feel like a small, light-weight handbag. The nurse came and removed it again yesterday. So I am glad to report that there is a cure for the sickness.

The chemo takes about an hour to inject into my system via a (diluting) drip. I can't even bring myself to look at the collection of syringes lined up for my—er—edification. Suffice to say that one is coloured bright red—this has implications further down the line, if you see what I mean, but we'll not go there! The hardest part for the nurse is finding a suitable vein in the fore-arm. I never mind all the needles, but I do begin to get apprehensive when I see her futile hunt along the length and breadth of my left forelimb.

Once it's over, you're free to go, with your bag of tablets. At this stage, you just want to get home as quickly as possible, though the rush-hour traffic makes this a forlorn hope.

The next few days are a bit rough, but bearable. I just lounge around, sleep, watch The Vicar of Dibley yet again, and still laugh! And eat often—which always helps me to feel better. Oh, and let Maureen do the ironing and half-a-dozen other things like walking the dog. Then the creative juices start flowing again, and I have to spend a little therapeutic time at the computer......Aaaah!!

Next dose is scheduled for 5th Nov at 8.50 am. Then I will have reached the half-way mark, DV! All the best to you all
Helen


## PRAYER

Father, not only has this cancer diagnosis been a terrible blow; but the weaponry designed to treat it can sometimes feel like another, heavier assault on my weakened flesh. Please help me to be patient and accepting, in the knowledge that the chemotherapy is going to war against the disease, on my behalf. Please may your angels guard me and strengthen me, that I may come through this treatment unscathed, and gloriously free of the cancer that has attacked my very being. In Jesus' name. Amen.

# POWER IN THE BLOOD!!

*Whoever eats my flesh and drinks my blood has eternal life, and I will raise him up at the last day.* John 6:54 (NIV)

*In him we have redemption through his blood, the forgiveness of sins, in accordance with the riches of God's grace.* Ephesians 1:7 (NIV)

*These are they that have come out of the great tribulation; they have washed their robes and made them white in the blood of the Lamb.* Revelation 7:14 (NIV)

Chemotherapy can have many side-effects, and some of them are cumulative (they build up over the course of chemo). I was therefore not surprised to be told, just before receiving my final dose, that my haemoglobin was low and that I would therefore need a blood transfusion. I could actually have told them this myself, as I had been feeling very limp and lacking in energy over the previous week or so.

I had the transfusion a few days later, eventually receiving two units. As it takes each unit two hours to infuse, that took a total of four hours altogether! After every last droplet of vital fluid had dripped into my veins, I was already feeling much stronger, and very thankful to the two anonymous donors, whose blood had so powerfully recharged my batteries.

Then, as I lay in bed that night, reflecting on the day's events, the words of an old missionary chorus sprang into my head. It was 'Power in the Blood'. The chorus is all about the heavenly, spiritual power we derive from the Blood of Jesus:

There is power, power,
Wonder-working power
In the precious blood of The Lamb.'

The Blood which Jesus shed for us on the cross has a much greater, and more permanent power than the two units I received in the hospital. As the hymn says, it has the power to take away our 'burden of sin'; to help us defeat evil; power over death; and above all, power to grant eternal life to all who believe in His Name!

And it was that heavenly power that I was able to tap into throughout my breast cancer illness and subsequent treatment. Right from the day of my diagnosis, I felt that God was with me, carrying me along. In fact, I have never felt His presence as much in my life as during those succeeding months of treatment. He really did take away the natural fear that anyone with a cancer diagnosis is bound to have. Through everything that happened I never really felt fear, which is amazing, considering what a hospital-phobic I am!

What was my reaction to the diagnosis? Well, on arriving home, I immediately asked God to help me through the unknown and uncertain future. I then prayed that as much good could come out of my situation as possible. Then I thought of my father, Harry, and my grandfather, John Long, both of whom held bravery awards. And the two of them became my inspiration. If I could only emulate their courage in my own personal fight with this disease, then I might feel worthy of their name.

And God answered my prayers in a wonderful way. He gave me the strength to face each hurdle along the journey. Well into my treatment, a neighbour remarked that seeing me took the fear out of cancer. If that was so, then that in itself was doing some good. I can also testify to the hugely beneficial effect the prayers of so many people, especially in the churches where I belong or am known, had on my recovery. To God alone be the glory!

## PRAYER

Heavenly father, whose son Jesus willingly shed His precious blood for me, help me to trust in the redeeming power of that blood; and give me the strength I need to face this disease and its treatment with fortitude and courage. In Jesus' name. Amen.

# MEASURING UP

*For You formed my inward parts;*
*You covered me in my mother's womb.*
*I will praise You, for I am*
*Fearfully and wonderfully made.*
Psalm 139 :13-14

I don't suppose many women get the chance of lying on a couch and having two pleasant professional men draw all over their bare bosom! Well, believe it or not, that was the position I found myself in one day in The Cancer Centre! And before you ask, it wasn't a game of Noughts and Crosses, although it might easily have been! I commented that I hoped it wasn't graffiti! Then along came the nurse with her digital camera and photographed the final effect! Would this mean instant stardom for Yours Truly? Could it even lead to playing opposite Richard Armitage in a romantic costume drama? (Oops, totally forgot I'm a pensioner of 60!)

Of course, the men in question were the Consultant and Registrar in the Radiotherapy Department, and in spite of all their sophisticated technology, they still needed to use a basic, little six-inch ruler for some of their measurements! The Registrar was a pleasant young man called Dr Rooney (Wayne's older, cleverer, better-looking brother, I joked!) He was very positive and encouraging about the beneficial effects of radiotherapy, which was good to hear. It, plus the chemo, plus the hormone therapy will all give me a very good chance for the future, he and his colleagues say.

After all the tattoos had been done, I was ushered into several other rooms with different amazing machines to accurately gauge and plot the measurements. This was all totally painless. Then we finished with a CT scan, and all was thus set up, ensuring that it should be fairly quick and straightforward, once the actual treatments started.

## PRAYER

Loving heavenly Father and Maker of all, I am truly amazed at your awesome creative power. My own body is a wonderful work of art, and now when something has gone wrong, you are providing the technology and expertise to fix it. Bless all those who work in the field of radiology, and especially the individuals tasked with my treatment. In Jesus' name. Amen.

# RADIATION

*From Thee all skill and science flow,*
*All pity, care and love,*
*All calm and courage, faith and hope;*
*O pour them from above. (C Kingsley)*

The Radiation Therapy experience is very different from the chemotherapy one. For a start, they are not injecting killer chemicals into your blood-stream; so there are none of the nasty side-effects associated with that. I found nothing to be scared of in radiation treatment. Possibly the worst aspect is the rather undignified way I had to lie, top-half commando, on the 'Super-Bed', with both arms raised behind my head on the blue arm-rests provided. But this is nothing. And you feel and see nothing as the radiation is being delivered to the affected area via the gantry of the machine. There is just a brief buzzing noise.

The machines used to deliver the radiation are real state-of-the-art technology. Their proper name is Linear Accelerators (LINAC), which makes me think of that great Particle Accelerator at Cerne in Switzerland! In my case, of course, the intention was not to find the God-particle; although as a Christian, I might have hoped that the evidence of my faith would have become obvious somewhere along the way!

A couple of weeks into the regime, the only visible evidence on my body was the reddening of the skin where the radiation was doing its job. This became progressively worse, but was managed very well over the six-week period by a wonderful band of nurses, with their arsenal of creams and ointments. As my skin got redder, they simply 'upped the anti'. I ended up with a Mepil….something gauze, and was well strapped up with silicone pads, which hadn't a great effect on my upper outline, but certainly helped with the all-important job of healing! I was really touched, to the point of tears, by the gentle and caring way these nurses treated my burnt skin. It very much reminded me of a mother tenderly applying a soothing salve to the skin of her injured child. Those were, indeed, healing hands in every sense of the word!

## PRAYER

Dear Father, thank-you for inspiring men and women to research and discover wonderful new ways of treatment and healing in the medical field. Thank-you for the precision and expertise involved in delivering the exact dose of radiation to the right area, without harming any other vital part of the body. And I bless you for the dedication of the nurses who work with cancer patients; let them know that their vocation is appreciated and really making a difference. In Jesus' name. Amen.

# SISTERLY SUPPORT SERVICE

*Peace I leave with you; my peace I give to you; not as the world gives do I give to you. Let not your hearts be troubled, neither let them be afraid.* John 14:27

As we confront the impact of cancer on our lives, where would we be without certain special people, who are there for us, playing a very important and necessary supportive role. For me, it has been the constant love and presence of my sister, Maureen. It was in this close relationship of sisterhood through the illness and treatment that I really came to experience and draw strength from Maureen's God-given qualities of compassion and support, as she journeyed alongside me all the way from Diagnosis Day until the Final Radiotherapy Session, eight months on.

As I coped with the rigours of the treatments and their effects on my body, so much of my mind was inevitably focused on Me, the Cancer Patient, that at times I know I must have taken Maureen, the Sister/Carer, for granted. But where would I have been without her through all those weeks and months of constant hospital visits? Apart from driving me there, sometimes very early in the morning, the loving presence of another sympathetic person, especially during chemotherapy, was invaluable—nay— indispensable! Coming from a small family as we do, Maureen was 'It', and never once complained about anything, even taking the dog for morning walks when I wasn't able. All this on top of running her own home and family, and continuing her church work as Lay Reader and Pastoral Assistant; as well as putting other things in her life on hold.

Not only that, but in the middle of my treatment regime, she herself was diagnosed with Type Two Diabetes, and had a steep learning curve ahead of her as she battled to come to terms with the implications of this for her whole way of life.

I benefited so much from Maureen's presence in my life during that year, and came to see and experience at first hand her wonderful, gentle compassion. Yet I may have tended to overlook the understandable strain and stress that she herself must actually have been enduring, as together we confronted and coped with every stage of my treatment. I know she was instrumental in my ability to cope with the many challenges of the situation, and in my ultimate recovery or remission, or whatever term you are supposed to use with this disease. Although sisters, we are very different people; always have been; always will be. But in the areas where it really matters, we have a sisterly solidarity; an enduring closeness, friendship and mutual care for each other's wellbeing, for which I am exceedingly grateful.

## PRAYER

Dear Father, thank-you for____, who is always there for me. Thank-you for the wonderful gift of our close relationship. Forgive me if I sometimes take her/him for granted as I focus on my own health and feelings. Please bless her/him, and bring her/him the consolation and strength that only you can give to the anxious and heavy-laden. In Jesus' name. Amen.

# TIME...

*For everything there is a season, and a time for every*
*matter under heaven:*
*a time to be born, and a time to die,*
*a time to plant, and a time to pluck up what has been planted;*
*a time to kill, and a time to heal...* (Ecclesiastes 3:1-3)

## THE PAGER

You will have to get used to The Pager,
And especially its *bleep*;
For the Bridgewater Suite and the Cancer Centre
Both make significant use
Of this mini flying-saucer.

The Pager's main function
Is to let you know when it's your turn to see somebody:
It could be to get bloods checked, to see the doctor,
Or to go for your infusion of chemotherapy,
Or for radiotherapy treatment.

Everyone is given a Pager on arrival,
So you get used to them 'going off' all around you.
They have a circle of flashing red lights, as well as
Their unique, unnerving bleep.

Sometimes you'll see
Stacks of them,
Briefly bleating in unison.

Of all my memories of the cancer treatment,
That unique, insistent bleep,
More than any other,
Has the power
Suddenly
To put me
Right back there.
Again.


## PRAYER

Thank-you, dear Father, for all the advances of modern
technology in the field of medicine, like the pagers used in the
hospital. Thank-you that they help with the efficient running of the
system, and that they save busy staff a lot of time and work. Please
help me to be patient as I wait for my turn to come, and to accept
that I will be called in due time. In Jesus' name. Amen.

# FELLOW TRAVELLERS

*Bear one another's burdens, and so fulfil the law of Christ.*
Galatians 6:2

*Brother, sister, let me serve you,*
*Let me be as Christ to you,*
*Pray that I may have the grace to*
*Let you be my servant too. (Richard Gilliland in Church Hymnal)*

Waiting for the radiation treatment can sometimes feel like a bit of a drag, but the radiographers are working under such pressure, with a constant flow of patients, that you can only feel sympathetic, supportive and grateful towards them. The very modern waiting area is a vast space, capable of seating around 50 people in its rows of chairs, arranged along the walls and down the centre of the room. There are seldom many free spaces, which tells its own story. It can be a bit like a game of Musical Chairs, although the only music comes from the little round pagers every patient receives on arrival, and the odd mobile phone going off.

Towards the end of my six-week stint I began to recognise people who were also attending every day at around the same time. It gave me a great feeling of solidarity, as I contemplated that we were all on the same journey together. And talking of journeys…..There was a small group of lovely, gentle people with whom I seemed to make a special connection. They were three couples who travelled by train every day all the way from Derry/Londonderry—a two-hour journey each way! On the few occasions I attended alone, they befriended me, and we quickly struck up a strong rapport. They were even interested in my knitting! I will never forget them and their warmth and kindness, most especially Marilyn, whose little memento I still cherish.

Indeed, meeting other patients was one of the pleasures of my RT experience. On another of my solitary days, I went into the busy café for a snack, and found myself sharing a table with a friendly lady from Dublin, now living in Northern Ireland. As we got chatting, she told me she was 87 and had had an operation for breast cancer some time before me. She explained that after her diagnosis she had been amazed to be offered a mastectomy at her advanced age. But she was told that everything was taken into consideration—her general health etc—and she was deemed eligible for the surgery. There she was, having made a great recovery, looking and sounding the picture of health, and planning to take up her swimming again. It was a real privilege to talk to such a lovely, positive person.

And finally, the Lady in the Lift. A total stranger, she confided, as we descended, that she had just been told she needed another breast operation, and was understandably very distressed. On emerging from the lift, I folded her in my arms in a big hug, which was, I judged, just what she needed at that time. As Christians, we all need to shed a little light on a troubled and darkened world.

## PRAYER

Heavenly Father, thank-you for the strangers who have become friends, or have even briefly touched my life as a result of cancer and its treatment. Thank-you for helping us to support one another. Please enable me to be open to the needs of others, many of whom are journeying along the same path as me. In Jesus' name. Amen.

The following extract is from United Christian Broadcasters' publication, 'The Word for Today', Nov, Dec 10, Jan 2011 issue.
www.ucb.co.uk
It appears with permission.

There's a bulletin board in a Mayo Clinic which reads:

## CANCER IS LIMITED
it cannot cripple love;
it cannot shatter hope;
it cannot erode faith;
it cannot eat away peace;
it cannot destroy confidence;
it cannot kill friendship;
it cannot shut out memories;
it cannot silence courage;
it cannot invade the soul;
it cannot reduce eternal life;
it cannot quench the spirit;
and it cannot lessen the power of the resurrection.

## YES, I CANCER
**Rhyme-time**
(Having some fun with THAT WORD)

Doctor, can you treat my cancer?
I am hoping that I can, sir.

What's the treatment for my cancer?
First, we'll have to do a scan, sir.

After that you'll treat my cancer?
That would be our cunning plan, sir.

What will help you treat my cancer?
Chemotherapy, if we can, sir.

Will it help to cure my cancer?
I can't give a definite answer.

Will we ever conquer cancer?
Let's be hopeful that we can, sir.

Now that we've discussed my cancer,
Thank-you for your truthful answers—
Let us act upon your plan, sir:
Do your best to cure this cancer!

# ISOLATION

## LOST

*He shall defend thee under his wings, and thou shalt be safe under his feathers.* Psalm 91:4

*What man of you, having a hundred sheep, if he has lost one of them, does not leave the ninety-nine in the wilderness, and go after the one which was lost, until he finds it? And when he has found it, he lays it on his shoulders, rejoicing.* Luke 15:3-5

Going through cancer treatment, possibly unable to get out as much due to debilitating side-effects, can make the sufferer feel isolated and cut-off, especially if living alone (like me). I felt particularly cut off from church, not managing to get out to a service for a period of five months. Yes, some good friends called, rang or wrote, but what of the silent majority? Did they even bother to think about me—these people among whom I had worshipped Sunday by Sunday over the years? No doubt some prayed, for which I am very grateful. But it was the not knowing whether the congregation as a whole was supporting me or not that really undermined me. So I wrote this poem:

## LOST FOR WORDS

I'm trying to find
The right word
To describe my Situation—
I think it probably needs to begin
With either Dis- or Ex-
But it isn't
Disestablishment
And it's definitely not
Excommunication!
Perhaps Disconnection
Or maybe Dislocation
Would better capture the sense of it…
A word to describe how you feel
When you're Out of Circulation
For months on end
Because you have cancer,
And are going through the mangle of chemotherapy…
When church life is going on as normal,
But you're no longer part of it—
Even worse—
If you live alone—
Exacerbation.
Contacts from a few, wonderful,
Special people,
Who have stayed the course,
Bring boundless blessings
Celebration!
But there is still this sense
Of being ill-and-cut-off—
Ill-solation?

Perhaps this is enough
Expostulation—
Maybe you will be able to
Help me find the right word—
The elusive one—

Commun...

## PRAYER

Lord Jesus, though all the world forsake me, I know that you
will not. You are my rock, my stronghold: let me hold on to you
at times when I feel isolated and alone. Help me to know that you
will not let this lost sheep go missing from your fold. Hide me
under the shadow of your wings. In your own dear name. Amen.

# YOU PUT YOUR RIGHT ARM IN !

*'Just as the body is one and has many members, and all the members of the body, though many, are one body, so it is with Christ.'*
1 Cor 12:12 (NRSV)

St. Paul is writing to the church in Corinth and he says that we are a team. He doesn't compare us to a football team or a rugby team but to the human body. Some of us are hands, says St. Paul, some of us are eyes, some of us are toes. BUT ALL OF US ARE IMPORTANT. Every one of us has a place.

Some of you reading this may know only too well how it feels when one part of your body or the body of a loved one is invaded by cancer. It actually affects our whole body, not just that isolated part. It affects how we feel, how we act, how we behave in the presence of others.

We are all important in the work of Christ. There are no first or second class citizens in the Christian community, the body of Christ. Even if you have cancer, God still has a work for you to do and a witness for you to make. It doesn't matter if you are a street cleaner or have risen to the highest position in your profession, we are all equally important and we all matter in the work to which Christ calls us. The hand cannot say to the foot, *'I have no need of you.'* And the foot cannot say to the eyes, *'I have no need of you.'* We all need each other and we all are equally important.

I wonder how many of you remember The Lone Ranger on television? What did you call the actor? Clayton Moore. I can remember the name of the actor who played Tonto because it is such a lovely name, JAY SILVERHEELS and what did he call the Lone Ranger? Yes KeMO SABe!!

Well you see, part of the problem is that there are too many what we might call "Lone Ranger" Christians. These Lone Rangers think they can serve Christ without being part of the team. They think they can deal with illness all on their own without Christ.

Just me, myself and I. But this is far from the Biblical ideal. Biblically, to be a follower of Christ is to be part of a family, part of a body, as it were. Metaphorically we are the body of Christ even if our own body has been invaded by cancer.

Ask yourself how you can use this cancer for good, how you can turn it around and make it a blessing to yourself and to others. My sister achieved this by producing a booklet of poems and meditations which she composed throughout her cancer treatment. This little book has raised £1200 for cancer charities. She had everyone in stitches (sorry for the pun) laughing at her multi-coloured punk wig which she donned in the cancer centre in the days before Christmas. She even sang Christmas Carols during chemotherapy.

# A PRAYER FOR USE IN HOSPITAL
by Rita Snowden

*My visitors have gone, O God, leaving me flowers, fruit*
*and magazines-and*
*For these I am thankful;*
*They have left me also, fresh things to think about...*
*But now I am tired...Save me from self-pity...Establish my faith*
*Within serenity, O God; strengthen my memory, that I can*
*hold on to what I know;*
*Sustain those I love at home and all whose days are now different;*
*Give me your sweet gift of sleep this night, refreshing and*
*calm. And bless all who labour to lighten the lot of others*
*in need. In Christ's name. Amen.*

# GREETINGS CARDS

I was amazed to read recently that each adult in the UK sends on average 55 greetings cards per year. That seemed rather a lot, but when I thought about Christmas, Birthday and 'Thank You' cards, and, of course, the 'Get Well' cards that we send when our friends or family are ill, I began to see that 55 cards might indeed be a realistic number for some people to send. This represents a lot of friendship and love and reminded me of the advice that I received from an elderly friend. She said that: our days are happier if we give people a piece of our heart, rather than a piece of our mind.

When I visit patients in hospitals their bedside lockers are often covered with cards from well wishers, all hoping that they soon recover from their ailment. However, on a psychiatric ward, one lady I was with showed me her solitary card. She said that she was the only person on her ward to have been sent a Get Well card. She was very touched by the fact that she was in someone's thoughts as she had been in hospital for some months. Her sense of isolation was broken by receiving that card, and it was a visible reminder that she was not forgotten and that she was loved.

Your diagnosis may have left you feeling very alone, but God has said, *'I will never leave you nor forsake you.'* When we feel really alone we should hold onto these words and those of the Psalmist who said of God:

*"If I rise on the wings of the dawn, if I settle on the far side of the sea, even there your hand will guide me, your right hand will hold me fast"*. Psalm 139:9 (NIV)

## A PRAYER FOR TODAY

Loving Father, thank you for the doctors and nurses who have been so kind, especially when they had to tell me that I have cancer. Strengthen them, and give them refreshment from the constant telling difficult news to patients. Bless their work and encourage them all to hope in you, through Jesus Christ our Lord. Amen.

# LONELY FURROW

All alone?

*"Turn to me and be gracious to me, for I am lonely and afflicted."*
Psalm 25:16 (NIV)

I live in the country and often watch what is going on in the farms round about. Each season brings its own interesting scenes. At harvest time, even though the farms are mechanised, the fields have a number of people there helping to gather in the crops. It is when the fields are being ploughed that there seems to be only one person, the driver in the tractor, pulling the plough across the land. Perhaps that is where we get the phrase, 'ploughing a lonely furrow' from. It is a solitary occupation that needs only one person. There are times in life when we are in a 'lonely furrow'. We are all on our own as it were. In the area of suffering this is often so. Friends and relations may take us to our hospital appointments. They may even come and sit with us, waiting until we are ready to go home, and that is great to have such good support, but in a real sense, we are alone. We are on a journey that we did not choose to travel. We are in a lonely furrow. The diagnosis does not refer to their body. The discussion of treatment does not impact their flesh. They cannot see the inner trembling or apprehension as the prognosis is spelt out. It is in that inner state that the depth of the furrow is felt.

# A PRAYER FOR TODAY

Dear God, thank you for the doctor who told me the news. I feel sorry for him as he has to tell so many people this sort of stuff. I hope that he looks to you, because he will need your strength and compassion to do his work well. Give him a great sense of your presence with him in his work and bless him richly, for Jesus' sake. Amen.

# A SEA OF PRAYER

*No man is an island. (John Donne)*
*What a friend we have in Jesus. (Joseph Scriven)*

I defy anyone to go through cancer and its treatment on their own. You need other people. Beginning with family, naturally. Then there are the doctors, nurses and radiographers who are closely involved in your treatment. And, of course, there are your friends, near and far. It was the support of these friends that I found to be of enormous significance throughout my treatment and during the recovery period. I sincerely believe they made a powerful contribution to the whole healing process, by their constancy and moral support.

During treatment, I was able to meet up with some; though as I found visits tiring, these were kept to a minimum. There were other people who phoned me regularly or sent text messages; one lady especially texting me before each session of chemotherapy (much appreciated). There were many, many cards, and I have kept them all! Amazingly, there are only two duplicates in the whole bunch!

Looking at them again, I marvel at how carefully chosen they all were, in order to match up with my personality and interests. Thus, there is a collection of dogs, butterflies and flowers that any municipal park would be proud of! How thoughtful of these people to select the type of cards that would most appeal to me! One friend always sent me a really quirky card to coincide with each chemotherapy session: they inevitably made me laugh and lifted my spirits.

Others wrote encouraging letters, or sent special cards at Christmas time. I even have one signed by a group of my old school chums, as they travelled on the Belfast-Londonderry train! I had intended to go with them, but found myself in hospital having surgery instead. Two RSPB colleagues took me out for lunch before Christmas. People were so kind. Not only was I being prayed for regularly in my own church, but also every Sunday in the one I used to belong to. After I had recovered, I went back there and personally thanked them for their faithfulness in prayer on my behalf: it definitely aided my healing and recovery. Another good friend, who lives in Merseyside, lit a candle regularly for me in her parish church. How I valued her commitment, prayers and cheering letters!

## PRAYER

Father, at this time especially, thank-you for friendship, in all its different forms and manifestations. Help me to be open to the kindness and support that my friends offer so freely, and I pray that you will bless them individually, as they continue to pray for me or to show their good wishes in whatever ways they think best. And thank-you that the best friend I could ever have is with me, and will support me all along the way, if I only put my trust in Him. Amen.

# FROM DESPAIR TO HOPE

## TIME FOR TEA?

*O taste and see that the Lord is good.*
*Happy is the man who takes refuge in him!* Psalm 34:8

One aspect of chemotherapy that can be quite severe is how your mouth and sense of taste are affected. For instance, I found it very hard to eat Prawn Cocktail on Christmas Day, because the acidic sauce really stung my palate. This is mostly a short-term problem, but the one thing that really got to me was how an ordinary cup of tea could taste so awful. What had been one of the most consoling things in my life was now laced with disgust—how very disquieting! Here is how I summed it up in December 2009:

When?
Oh when?
Oh when?
Oh when
Will tea taste normal again?

When?
Oh when?
Oh when?
Oh when
Will tea taste normal again?

Thankfully, after the completion of chemotherapy, my taste slowly returned to something approaching normal. However, ever since, I have become very discerning about tea flavours, and what I like and dislike; though I do make a point of supporting Fair Trade brands. Anyone for tea?

## PRAYER

Father, thank-you for the adequate provision of food and water in our land, and for all its subtle and contrasting flavours. I pray that you will help me to cope now, when things don't taste as they should. And please remember those who do not have enough even for one square meal a day. Please help us out of our plenty to relieve world hunger. In Jesus' name. Amen.

# TRACE THE RAINBOW

*"We are hard pressed on every side, but not crushed; perplexed, but not in despair; persecuted, but not abandoned; struck down, but not destroyed."*
2 Corinthians 4:8,9 (NIV)

There are times when things look very dark indeed, so dark that we have to struggle to find hope. In the waiting for any signs of hope there is even more pain, and nothing else to do but try to wait patiently.

George Matheson was just fifteen when he was told that he was going to become totally blind. However he was not going to be defeated and enrolled in Glasgow University, later graduating in 1861. His sisters were a great support to him in his pursuit of theology, and even studied Greek, Hebrew and Latin in order to be of help to him. Despite their care for him they could not mend his broken heart when his fiancée broke off their engagement, because she felt that she could not face the challenges of life with a man who was blind. Later, when one of his sisters married, her wedding brought back painful memories of his personal heart-break, and in despair he reached out in faith to lay hold on the unchanging love of God. This unchanging love, he wrote of as, 'a love that wilt not let me go'. In this he wrote four verses of his most famous hymn.

O Love that wilt not let me go,
I rest my weary soul in thee;
I give thee back the life I owe,
That in thine ocean depths its flow
May richer, fuller be.

O light that foll'west all my way,
I yield my flick'ring torch to thee;
My heart restores its borrowed ray,
That in thy sunshine's blaze its day
May brighter, fairer be.

O Joy that seekest me through pain,
I cannot close my heart to thee;
I trace the rainbow through the rain,
And feel the promise is not vain,
That morn shall tearless be.

O Cross that liftest up my head,
I dare not ask to fly from thee;
I lay in dust life's glory dead,
And from the ground there blossoms red
Life that shall endless be.

There are indeed times when things look very dark. It is like Job in the storm (Job 38:1ff); Abraham on the road to Moriah (Genesis 22); Moses in the desert of Midian (Exodus 2:11ff); or the Son of Man in the Garden of Gethsemane (Matthew 26:36ff). It takes real faith to 'trace the rainbow through the rain', but it also takes the storm-cloud to make the rainbow. The Psalmist would say: "Why are you downcast, O my soul? Why so disturbed within me? Put your hope in God, for I will yet praise him, my Saviour and my God." Psalm 42:11 (NIV)

# WHEN A CHILD GETS CANCER

"*The wolf also shall dwell with the lamb,*
*The leopard shall lie down with the young goat,*
*The calf and the young lion and the fatling together;*
*And a little child shall lead them.*"
Isaiah 11:6 (NKJV)

The only thing more devastating than adult cancer must surely be cancer in children. When a beloved child dies from cancer, it seems such a contradiction in terms. Children represent life in all its fullness—the hope of the next generation. But then we must remember that we are all part of this fallen, broken world, where tragedies occur, and bad things sometimes happen to good people.

No-one knows better than God just what it is to watch a child suffer and die, as His only Son did just that—willingly—for us, to save this fallen world:

*How deep the Father's love for us,*
*How vast beyond all measure,*
*That he should give His only Son*
*To make a wretch His treasure!*
*How great the pain of searing loss:*
*The Father turns his face away*
*As wounds which mar the chosen one*
*Bring many sons to glory!*
*(Stuart Townsend, Church Hymnal)*

Children are resilient. And the good news on the medical front is that many childhood cancers are curable; but not all. In my own experience I can think of a little girl of four, a teenage schoolboy, a little boy of five, and a toddler of two, all of whom lost their battles with cancer, to the everlasting anguish of their parents. Perhaps we can gain some consolation in the attitude of The Good Shepherd towards children:

*But Jesus said, "Let the little children come to me, and do not stop them; for it is to such as these that the kingdom of heaven belongs. And he laid his hands on them and went on his way."*
Matthew 19:14,15 (NRSV)

What wonderful reassurance is in these simple, yet emphatic words! We may be sure from them that Our Lord has a special love for the young, and if they should depart this earthly life, then they will find the warmest of welcomes from Him in heaven, where they will remain safe, happy and cherished, until we ourselves join them there.

*"And God will wipe every tear from their eyes. Death will be no more; mourning and crying and pain will be no more, for the first things have passed away."*
Revelation 21:4 (NRSV)

## PRAYER

Dear loving Lord God, I/we bring our child before you in humble prayer, asking that he/she might be healed. We pray that you will give our whole family the strength and resilience to face the days ahead, one at a time, and to put all our trust in you, that the treatments, although severe, might restore……..to health, and fullness of life. In Jesus' name. Amen.

# CHERRY BLOSSOM

The change from Spring to Summer is remarkably pretty, with the Cherry Blossom shedding its pale petals all over the ground, and the wind catching and blowing them into shallow drifts, like spilt confetti. It is a brief moment that we should grasp for it all too soon disappears from our view and thoughts; the ethereal beauty gone. In our world where, at the moment, the external challenges to succeed are so pressing, this pretty shower of cherry blossom can be disregarded along with thoughts of youth, even life itself, as a time of brief beauty; a passing moment...all gone. We wonder if any of our efforts really matter. Is there something in life that remains of all our strivings?

Science would tell us that nothing in nature, not even the tiniest particle, can disappear without trace. Nature doesn't know extinction. All it knows is transformation. I saw it happen last year in a profusion of nasturtiums. In one day the leaves were gone, and only stalks remained. Some very hungry caterpillars were at work, transforming the leaves to energy for their long incarceration in a chrysalis, before transformation to the butterfly.

Everything that I have learned from science points to this transforming principle, that nothing is lost without trace. Jesus said: *"And why do you worry about clothing? Consider the lilies of the field, how they grow; they neither toil nor spin, yet I tell you, even Solomon in all his glory was not clothed like one of these.'* (Mt 6:28 NRSV) God has applied these principles to these minute parts of his universe, which encourages us in our belief that we will have continuity in our spiritual existence after death.

107

## A PRAYER FOR TODAY

Dear Lord, help me to look beyond this moment to you. Please hold me through this confusion and fear, and bring your peace into my heart. Help me to show your peace to my family and friends who are too scared even to name their fears, for I ask in Jesus' name. Amen.

# YOU'LL NEVER WALK ALONE

*The Lord is my shepherd, I shall not be in want.*
*He makes me lie down in green pastures,*
*He leads me beside quiet waters; He restores my soul.*
*He guides me in paths of righteousness for his name's sake.*
*Even though I walk through the valley of the shadow of death,*
*I will fear no evil, for you are with me;*
*Your rod and your staff, they comfort me.*
*You prepare a table before me In the presence of my enemies.*
*You anoint my head with oil; my cup overflows.*
*Surely goodness and love will follow me all the days of my life,*
*And I will dwell in the house of the Lord for ever.* Psalm 23 (NIV)

A cancer diagnosis can bring us face to face with the ultimate reality of death. Yet for the Christian, even those whose faith is wavering and being tested now like never before, there is the assurance of a loving God, whose own Son knew what it was to feel fear and to suffer grievously, and who will never forsake us, through good or ill.

I am not a Liverpool fan, although I once owned and loved a dog named Shankley. But way back in the Swinging Sixties, I was a fan of Gerry and the Pacemakers, who immortalised that great song from 'Carousel', 'You'll Never Walk Alone'. Why is it still so popular, after all that time, while Gerry & Co have long faded from the limelight? Well, it embodies the noble idea of courage, whatever the difficult circumstances. The words and music, surging to a crescendo, are in many ways inspirational:

'When you walk through a storm, hold your head up high,
And don't be afraid of the dark;
At the end of a storm, there's a golden sky,
And the sweet, silver song of a lark.
Walk on through the wind, walk on through the rain,
Though your dreams be tossed and blown;
Walk on, walk on, with hope in your heart,
And you'll never walk alone,
You'll never walk alone!'

Hope is the backbone of the song; and it is something that we need in large amounts at this time of serious medical diagnosis; and particularly in the face of our own mortality. It is a positive attribute and is mentioned often in the Bible. In 1 Corinthians 13, Saint Paul names Faith, Hope and Love as the three enduring attributes to own or aspire to. Hope is something that we should ask God for now, as we seek His help to be positive through this cancer journey.

With God (who is the essence of all hope) in our hearts, we will never walk alone; for even through the valley of the shadow of death, He will be journeying with us, and often carrying us, when the going gets too tough. He will never fail us nor forsake us, whatever happens.

## PRAYER

Dear Lord Jesus, right now I don't know what the future holds for me. I need to feel your risen presence very near to me at this time, reassuring me and giving me hope. Please walk with me through the storm of illness that is battering me at the moment. You, who commanded the wind and waves to be still, please take my hand and lead me safely through whatever I may have to face. In Your Name. Amen.

# LAUGHTER? IN THIS CONTEXT? YOU MUST BE JOKING!

*"When the Lord restored the fortunes of Zion,*
*We were like those who dream.*
*Then our mouth was filled with laughter,*
*And our tongue with shouts of joy."*
Psalm 126: vs 1-2

A sense of humour, I have found, can help you through many testing situations. It oils the cogs of inter-person relationships, and I found it indispensable during my 33 years as a teacher.

But surely, you say, the words 'humour' and 'cancer' must be, by their very nature, mutually exclusive. From experience I haven't found it to be so. I quickly discovered that the more effort I made to find humour in even the least pleasant aspects of the cancer and its treatment, the better I and those around me were able to deal with it. The high point of this was the multi-coloured punk wig I wore to the hospital for my penultimate chemo, the week before Christmas. As with any 'costume', as soon as I put it on, I felt like a different person. I felt like: OK, I'm bald, but this is what I'm doing about it. This is Helen Long giving the two fingers to No Hair Day!

I watched as the smiles spread across the faces of staff and patients alike, and many conversations ensued. While I received the infusion of Taxotere, I sang Christmas Carols quietly to myself.

At home, especially during the tiring latter months of treatment,

I kept my spirits up on a constant diet of 'The Vicar of Dibley'. I found that, no matter how many times I watched the episodes, I could still find them amusing and uplifting.

I believe that laughter deserves its place in the Medicine Cabinet just as much as the more conventional bottles on the shelves. It is a great antidote to stress, even in the otherwise healthy, and can help the healing process and bring about a more positive frame of mind. Below is one of the 'hairy limericks' I wrote about the inevitable hair-loss:

*The advantage of losing my hair—*
*My brains are exposed to the air—*
*The cobwebs have gone,*
*The lights have come on,*
*And poetry's filling the air!*

## PRAYER

Dear loving Father, our creator and sustainer: thank-you for the gift of laughter, even in the most trying of circumstances. I pray that you will open my heart and my mind to the glimpses of light that laughter brings, and that you will enable that light to shine on and through me and my loved-ones as we journey along this rough and rocky road. In Jesus' precious name. Amen.

# POPPY POWER

*The flowers appear on the earth; The time of singing has come,*
*And the voice of the turtledove Is heard in our land.*
Song of Solomon 2:12

Picture a car-park at a Leisure Centre. Picture a quiet grassy corner at the back, which the Council had tilled in preparation for planting something and then forgotten about. Then watch me as I decide to give it a bit of experimental flower-power. It is very easy, probably the easiest bit of gardening I have ever done. And cheap, too. The price of a packet of poppy seeds (Ladybird), which I sprinkle over the bed, roughly rake in, and leave the rest to nature. I smile as I drive away, thinking of my little secret.

I wasn't smiling a few months later, when I was told I had aggressive breast cancer, and the seeds were all but forgotten. Much happened over the succeeding weeks, culminating in a lumpectomy on 14th August and a spell of recovery in hospital. On arriving home, once I had regained some strength, I wanted to get back out again, to the Leisure Centre, where I usually walk the dog. So Maureen took me, though I didn't walk very far that first day. As Maureen walked on with the dogs, I looked around me, and what a sight greeted my dazzled eyes! The poppies were blooming in the sun and a myriad of insects were buzzing around them, delighting in the freely available nectar. How wonderful! How it lifted my spirits, as I looked around me at the rest of God's beautiful world, smiling in the August sunshine! The poem was inspired by what I saw. *(By the way, the eagle-eyed may have spotted an unintended pun earlier in this paragraph!)*

## POPPIES

*(For Maureen)*
Poppies red, poppies red,
In the secret flower-bed.

Honey-bee, honey-bee,
Runny, runny-honey-bee

Hover-fly, hover by—
Here's another hover-fly!

Leaf-weevil, leaf-weevil—
Chlorophyll thief-weevil!

Hawk in flight, hawk in flight,
Swept by swallows out of sight!!

Poppies red, poppies red,
Healing from this flower-bed!

## PRAYER

Dear Father, creator of all that lives and breathes on our planet, thank-you for the bright, unexpected gifts you bestow on us. Teach us to find beauty and encouragement in the small things we see—that even something as small as a hoverfly is a wonder of nature. And in our darkest, weakest moments, give us hearts that are open to your healing love, wherever it may manifest itself. In Jesus' name. Amen.

# FLYING HIGH

Lift me to soar high again.

*...but those who hope in the LORD will renew their strength. They will soar on wings like eagles; they will run and not grow weary, they will walk and not be faint.* Isaiah 40:31 (NIV)

I often watch the birds on the shore of Strangford Lough. From my observation point I can see crows in large numbers rising from the trees on the island opposite. It might be more accurate to say that I hear them first, because they announce their presence with a cacophony of laughter and argument. They love nothing more than a windy day, when they can play in the conflict of air currents, rising and riding the air as it flows over the water. Yes, they are crows, and I don't expect to see eagles there, but even the crows understand their surroundings and how to use their environment, not just to survive, but to take pleasure in creation. From the same place I have also observed buzzards, sometimes high over the fields surveying them for their prey, and on windy days turning at height in the thermals. It is spectacular to see the way they use the currents of wind to maintain their elevation without seeming effort. Even having had the aerodynamics of flight explained to me I still gaze in wonder at the awesomeness of nature. Without wings and flight feathers we are very much earth-bound creatures, and when times are difficult we can feel as though we are filled with lead and everything demands so much effort. Even our very spirits seem to be held down. Isaiah tells us that when *we hope in the Lord we will renew our strength. We will soar on wings like eagles; we will run and not grow weary, we will walk and not be faint.* He wants us to put things into a divine perspective; to hope in the Lord. The eagle appears fearless in the storm, rising with the wind and drawn up by cloud to heady heights. We need to take a change of air, metaphorically speaking, and get out our wings to rise above the ugliness of our disease and burdens which hold us down. We need to breathe the fresh air of the heavenlies, by letting our Lord, the Omnipotent One, renew us in spirit and strength for the daily battle.

## A PRAYER FOR TODAY

Father God, I long to soar like an eagle, to be lifted up and free of all that holds me down in mere existence. Fill me with your Holy Spirit and lift me out of myself to look to you for renewal and refreshment. Lord, renew my body, mind and spirit and bring me new strength in you, for I ask in Jesus' name. Amen.

# LOSING HAIR, BUT NOT LOSING HEART

*Are not two sparrows sold for a copper coin? And not one of them falls to the ground apart from your Father's will. But the very hairs of your head are numbered. Do not fear therefore; you are of more value than many sparrows.* Matthew 10: 29-30 (NKJV)

### FACING IT IN THE MIRROR
Whose is this
Strange
Unfamiliar
Face
Staring back at me,
Minus its soft, feminine frame of hair?

'It's me! It's me!
It's me!' I cry
Striving somehow to retain
My sense of self
The comfortable 'me'
I always—until now—
Have recognised—
My very own
Familiar
Identity.

## AUTUMN

It is autumn
And I watch the leaves drift down
The trees will soon be bare—
A necessary loss
To survive the ravages of winter

And I, too, with loss of hair
And head that's bare—
Another necessary loss
To survive my winter ravages.

Come spring
We should all
In time
Be fresh in bud and leaf again!


## A PRAYER

Dear Lord God, creator and sustainer of us all, I feel even more vulnerable, now that I have lost my hair. Teach me to remember that to you, I am just the same as I ever was, and help me to remember this myself, too. Please help me to be patient, and to have faith that, after the chemotherapy, my hair will grow back as good as new again. In Jesus' name. Amen.

# TRUSTING GOD

## JESUS ROCKS!

*In thee, O Lord, have I put my trust: let me never be put*
*to confusion, deliver me in thy righteousness.*
*Bow down thine ear to me: make haste to deliver me.*
*And be thou my strong rock, and house of defence, that*
*thou mayest save me.*
*For thou art my strong rock, and my castle: be thou also my*
*guide, and lead me for thy Name's sake.....*
*Into thy hands I commend my spirit: for thou hast redeemed*
*me, O Lord, thou God of truth.*
Psalm 31 (Book of Common Prayer, 1926)

Between a Rock and a Hard Place is a situation we all would
rather avoid.  But what if we can't avoid it?  What do we do then?

When I got my breast cancer diagnosis and needed a course of
chemotherapy, that is where I felt I was: caught between the rock of
cancer and the hard place of chemotherapy treatment that I knew
had a nasty reputation.

On reflection, rocks and stones have played a significant part
in my life (apart from the elusive one for the 3$^{rd}$ finger, left hand!).
The little, well-chosen stones from the roadside that were used in
our games of hop-scotch were the first. (No health & safety then!!)
Their size and shape, combined with our aim, had the power to
determine our success or failure in the game.  Then there was my

headlong teenage dash in pursuit of the Rolling Stones, across the railway lines behind the old GNR, as they dodged the mass of fans waiting at the front entrance. (Another huge health & safety issue here, on several counts!) Thankfully, I quickly recovered from that rocky phase.

And now, at Sensible-60, I am the proud owner of a little dog whose name is 'Pebbles', and I feel I have come full circle! Pebbles are lovely little rounded stones with no hard edges: which is probably a perfect description of my pet—a rounded body with no hard edges, apart from her exceedingly pointy ears.

Anyway, there I was, caught between the proverbial rock and hard place. What could I do? All I did was pray, and keep praying for strength to get through it all; and then I left it in God's hands. And do you know what? He hasn't let me down. I am coping with this not in my own poor strength, but through the Grace of God, who is our rock and our salvation.

Ask the Saviour to help you,
Comfort, strengthen and keep you;
He is willing to aid you;
He will carry you through.

Even better, and totally unexpectedly, I found myself being prompted to write about my experiences of this illness and treatment, again and again. Perhaps my poems and other writings will be the means of comfort, or at least light relief, for fellow sufferers, now and in the future. I can honestly say that in my ongoing journey through this illness and treatment, I have felt God's presence much more in my life than ever before. Perfect Love casts out fear. Apart from the initial shock of the diagnosis, I haven't really felt fear, or lost one night's sleep. Isn't that rather amazing in someone with cancer? Yes, it is indeed: Amazing Grace! To God be the glory!

I have also learned the deeper meaning of trust; not just in God, but in the wonderful way He uses the superb doctors and nurses in Belfast City Hospital. And I, who am so impatient, have had to learn patience. Along each step of this journey there is an inevitable period of waiting, often for important results that could affect your whole future, the most significant being the MRI scan. Some aspects of chemotherapy are not pleasant, but now such things as sickness can be well controlled, as I can testify. And isn't it great, it's there to go into battle on our behalf against the rogue cells invading our bodies?

I have also learned the joy of genuine friendship, love and support from so many people that I know, as well as the family. Their prayers and good wishes are like a raft, helping me to keep afloat. I have discovered so much goodness in people over the past few months, that I am just left speechless (maybe not a bad thing!). I even got a hug from the window-cleaner!

So, if you should happen to be ambushed by cancer, put your trust in Jesus, the Rock of Ages, and that will be sufficient; in fact, it will be more than enough. The two lines below, from the hymn 'Rock of Ages', brought me much comfort as I entered hospital for my operation, at the beginning of my journey:

Nothing in my hand I bring,
Simply to thy Cross I cling...

## A PRAYER

Lord Jesus, be my rock throughout this illness and treatment. Whatever I may have to face with this disease, let me always find shelter and refuge in your never-failing love and mercy. Amen.

# CROWS

As I write, the crows on the stony shore in front of my kitchen window make fascinating viewing. One crow carefully selects a mussel from the rocks and tries to break into its hard shell. When that doesn't work, he will take it in his beak and fly upwards, dropping the mussel from a height, and swooping down to see if it has cracked. Higher and higher he goes, time after time, until the shell fractures, and he is able to get the soft tasty shell fish inside. He is not on his own, for crows gather beneath him watching each time for the result of the impact as the mussel hits the stone. But they are not solely observers. They are opportunists; and they will jump in quickly to gain from the other's work to break open the shell. There is seldom a fight over division of labour. It is just accepted behaviour. Could it be that I am observing a school for crows, where the older ones are teaching some of their amazing skills?

To enjoy an abundant life we all need someone to learn from. The Psalmist said:

'*Show me your ways, O LORD, teach me your paths; guide me in your truth and teach me, for you are God my Saviour, and my hope is in you all day long*'. Psalm 25: 4,5 (NIV)

Jesus said:

"*Take my yoke upon you and learn from me, for I am gentle and humble in heart, and you will find rest for your souls. For my yoke is easy and my burden is light.*" Matthew 11:29 (NIV)

## A PRAYER FOR TODAY

Lord, I am desperate, give me a heart that wants to know you more, and help me to take every opportunity to come close to you, so that I may learn from you. I need that rest for my soul that you promise to all who seek you. Grow me in your grace, through Jesus Christ our Lord. Amen.

# SPRING CLEANING

The other day I was on the step ladder reaching for a book on the top shelf of the bookcase. It was dusty as it hadn't been visited for some time. Up there were books that had been bought because someone had recommended them, or because they were on a 'best sellers' list. Some had been read from cover to cover and put aside to read again; others were books that hadn't got off to a good start and had been filed away as difficult. Why don't I just get rid of them? Well they don't disturb me. They make the bookshelf look complete, rather than empty. I wonder how many books are shelved like that: read once; or opened and discarded after a brief trial.

Whatever 'Best seller' list we look at the Bible is still the best selling book of all time. Most households have at least one. Where is yours? Is it on the top shelf, out of the way where you don't disturb it and it doesn't disturb you, or is it readily assessible?

Do you search it regularly for words of comfort, or do you use it to help you in your daily living?

Read it! Let it disturb you, for within the pages of the Bible you will find God's eternal Word, unchanged and yet ever relevant. The Bible speaks to the turmoil, restlessness, chaos and discontent which is within our lives and gives us peace and hope for the future. St Paul put it this way in his letter to the Romans: *"Be transformed by the renewing of your mind."* Romans 12:2

## A PRAYER FOR TODAY

Dear Lord, I'm in difficulty and I need your help and reassurance. Help me to take up your book and really read it, and take it in. Little by little fill my spirit with your hope and love, through Jesus Christ our Lord. Amen.

# NESTING BOX

*But I trust in you, O LORD; I say, "You are my God." My times are in your hand; deliver me from the hand of my enemies and persecutors.*
Psalm 31:14,15a (NRSV)

It is a beautiful morning as I sit in my study looking out to one side over Strangford Lough, and in the other direction at the Mourne Mountains. The sun, although still low in the sky is shining on the water giving it the appearance of a million gems twinkling, while the sun on the slopes of Slieve Donard, the highest mountain in the range, makes the snow look so inviting. I have my notebook by my side and I am pondering in a timeless way, just gazing out of the window. It is late January and I note that the weather has been very mild so far through this winter. Almost as soon as the thought crosses my mind I am drawn to the flash of a bird flying into the nesting box under the eaves beside the window. It is a great tit. Hardly had I noted its presence till it was away again in a rush. There was such urgency about this little bird, lining its nest with dry moss in preparation for the laying of eggs. I wanted to tell it: "You're too early! You should wait a bit. The weather is milder than normal. Look at the snow on Slieve Donard."

I went to my bird book for information and found that, 'in Europe the breeding season usually begins after March, but the sunlight and daytime temperature also affects breeding time.' I also read that the incubation time is about two weeks.

126

The whole direction of my thoughts had been changed by the flash of this industrious little bird. I wondered how they would survive if the weather took a turn for the worse and winter finally arrived in full measure. All I could do was watch from the quiet vantage point of my study, and I mentally promised to make sure that the bird feeders were full every day and that water was in the bird bath; to do what I could to ease any harsh conditions.

Realisation dawned. We do not know what is round the corner for us, and that is a great mercy, because if we did, we would not live life to the full every day if we were expecting something unpleasant to happen to us. I'm sure that you never expected that you would be dealing with cancer, but here you are now right in this unimaginable situation, dealing with it day by day. You have support from many people, your doctors, nurses, ministers and support workers, to say nothing of family who are there anxiously waiting at your side. Along with those who are very visible in your treatment and care are many others, unknown to you, who are praying for your refreshment and recovery. It is a bit like my little eager birds making their nest in January, not knowing what the next few weeks will bring, nor do they know the commitment I have made to provide food and water for their sustenance. They carry on regardless. When I think of them I am drawn to the Psalmist's declaration: 'But I trust in you, O LORD; I say, "You are my God." My times are in your hand.' Psalm 31:14,15a

# PRAYER

Dear heavenly Father, increase my faith and trust in you, and help me to understand that my times are in your hands. Thank you for all the care I have received from the doctors, nurses, and support workers at the hospital, and from my family and friends. Banish all fear from around me and help me to rely on you, knowing that you have promised to never leave me or forsake me. Lift my eyes from my self pity to your face and give me grace for today. I ask this in Jesus' name. Amen.

# WEATHERING THE STORMS OF LIFE

*'But immediately Jesus spoke to the disciples and said, "Take heart, it is I; do not be afraid"'* Matthew 14:27

I happened to be in an evangelical shop a few weeks ago and, as I am always on the lookout for unusual and witty Tee shirts, I was delighted when I spied a white Tee shirt with a red cross on the front. The writing said, **'MY PHYSICIAN WALKS ON WATER'**! Yes, I bought it!

It's almost certain that we will never see anyone walking on water, so, in a literal sense, we cannot relate to the experience of the disciples in Matthew's accounts of Jesus' walking on the water. But, in a figurative sense, we have all experienced storms to varying degrees.

At this time, you, or a loved one, may be weathering the storm of a cancer diagnosis. When we get caught in a storm, it doesn't necessarily mean that we are off course, nor does it mean that God has forgotten us or has singled us out for punishment. The only thing we can say with certainty about storms is that they are a part of life, even for the best and most devout people on earth.

Isn't it strange to note that Jesus was the one who sent the disciples out in that boat? They were following His instructions when they got caught up in the storm on the Sea of Galilee. Surely this should tell us that, being a follower of Christ, leading a good life, doing the will of God, does not give us immunity from trouble. Sometimes, as you may be experiencing now, the very opposite is true. If Christians never became sick, then following Christ would not be an act of faith and devotion, it would be a business transaction, an insurance policy against disaster. As long as we live in this world, we are going to encounter unexpected turbulence but, as with the disciples, in the midst of the storm, Jesus came to his disciples and His presence made all the difference. He did not abandon them and he will not abandon us.

When the storm of sorrow comes, He will be there with words of comfort. When the storm of temptation comes, He will be there with words of strength. When the storm of guilt comes, He will be there with words of forgiveness. When the storm of discouragement comes, He will be there with words of hope. It is at the point where we are just about to faint, that God gives us the strength to go on. In the midst of life's storms of illness, if we look for Jesus we will see Him; if we listen we will hear Him say, *'Take heart, it is I; do not be afraid.'* I pray that, whatever suffering we have to face in this life, we will remember that Christ is with us and will never leave us. We will never be asked to bear more than we can. It was Corrie ten Boom who said, *'No matter how deep our darkness, Christ is deeper still'.*

Remember the beautiful diamond which started off as a lump of coal subjected to extreme pressure over a long period of time or the pearl which is created from an irritating object which the oyster covers with layer upon layer of smooth mother of pearl excreted from its own body.

God often uses our sufferings to reveal something beautiful and precious in our lives. In my sister Helen's case, it revealed her positive spirit which inspired her to write poems about her whole experience of breast cancer from start to finish. Her book raised over £1000 for Cancer Funds.

What will be revealed through your suffering? Will it make you a better person or a bitter person? Will it be a stumbling block or a stepping stone?

*'But Jesus immediately said to them, "Take courage! It is I. Don't be afraid."'*

## PRAYER

Heavenly Father, you are the source of all healing. I pray that I will feel your presence in the midst of this storm. I know you are always at my side and will never leave me. It's just that, sometimes, I am uncertain of your presence and it is then that I begin to doubt your promises. Persuade me that I should never doubt in the dark what you have promised in the light, that you are my unseen companion whom I can trust to carry me through this difficult time. Father, give me the courage not to be afraid! In the name of Jesus Christ my Saviour. Amen.

A calm Sea of Galilee at Tiberias in April 2009

# GOT YOUR SAT-NAV?

*"I am the way and the truth and the life."* John 14:6 (NRSV)

I am a lover of children's books, and Alice in Wonderland by Lewis Carroll is a great favourite of mine. In this there is a point when Alice encounters the Cheshire cat. It is smiling at her and she asks it: "Cheshire Puss, which way should I go?"

The cat replies, "Where do you want to get to?"

Alice responds, "I don't really care," to which the cat replies: "Then it doesn't matter which way you go!"

Of course, in life, it does matter which way we do go, and what direction we take. Nothing as important as a life decision should be determined on a whim or impulse. Jesus said, "I am the way and the truth and the life."

Suppose you were in a strange place and wanted to ask directions. Imagine that the person you speak to says: "Take the first to the right, and the second to the left. Then cross the square and the road that you want is the third on the left." You set off and you get lost before you reach the square. You then ask someone else, who says, "Come with me. I'll take you there." In this case for us that person is the way, and we do not miss it. That is what Jesus does for us.

Jesus also said, "I am the truth." The Psalmist says, "Teach me your way, O LORD, and I will walk in your truth." (Psalm 86:11) Jesus embodies truth.

A long time ago Thomas a Kempis wrote in his book 'Imitation of Christ', "Without the way there is no going, without the truth there is no knowing, without the Life there is no living."

Life with Jesus is a life worth living. In him alone we see what God is like. In him alone we have access to God. He can lead us into the presence of God without fear and without shame. It is about believing without seeing.

The truth is not just Jesus' utter dependability, but the saving truth of his gospel message.

'The way' speaks of the connectedness between two people or things – here the link between God and sinners. Truth reminds of the complete reliability of Jesus in all that he does and is. And 'Life' stresses the fact that mere physical existence matters little.

## A PRAYER FOR TODAY

My Lord and my God, give me grace to cast all my cares on you and follow your footsteps closely knowing that you will never lose me nor forsake me. Guide me into your path of life eternal, that I may rejoice regardless of what happens, through Jesus Christ our Lord. Amen.

# LESSONS FROM BIRDS

*I will sing of your strength, in the morning I will sing of your love;*
*for you are my fortress, my refuge in times of trouble. O my Strength,*
*I sing praise to you; you, O God, are my fortress, my loving God.*
Psalm 59:16,17 (NRSV)

You can see life from our windows. It's not that we live in a built up area, quite the opposite, but you see nature in the raw, and it encourages human comparisons. I delight in the bird life that frequents our garden and the surrounding fields and Lough shore, and have become an avid observer. Each season brings new sojourners to accompany us briefly on our journey, and enrich our appreciation of creation. Some are popular and loved, but others have a reputation which disinclines too much attention. This is a pity, as in life we have to take each person as we find them, and so it should be with all creation.

Take the starling for instance; it appears to be black, but closer attention shows that it is glossy with a deep sheen of purple and green, spangled with white. They are such noisy and gregarious birds, which utter both melodic and mechanical sounds to attract attention. Many people simply dismiss them, but they flock in an amazing manner and move in perfect synchrony, wheeling and turning at speed, outperforming many other species. Their motion has defied rational explanation, responding to one another's flight pattern in each murmuration and looking as though they strictly obey three basic rules: move in the same direction as your neighbour, remain close to them and avoid collisions.

This particular afternoon I watched their flock wheel and turn, eventually coming in to land on the overhead electric cables. A tight packed formation in flight became a close packed row on each electric line, swinging and fluctuating precariously. As each new bird joined the line-up the row bounced to and fro with the simple harmonic motion engendered in the cable. A thought struck me: each bird has an immense effect on those in close proximity to it. It was as though a light came on in my head: of course, that is exactly as it is with us. When we do something, those around us are affected by it. The same thing occurs when something happens to us. If we are afflicted by something difficult or complex then those close to us are also affected, and sometimes acutely.

When we hear that we have a diagnosis such as cancer, it touches us deeply, but perhaps because of our situation, we do not realise how it impinges on those close to us. We can well feel that we are on a tight rope which is swinging precariously, rather like the starling on the electric cable, but our loved ones can also feel perilously insecure. In attempts to hold on to our equanimity neither we nor they articulate our feelings for fear of falling in pieces. It is then that we need to turn to God and tell him of our feelings and fears, placing ourselves in his hands, and asking him for the blessing of knowing his presence very close to us. The Psalmist reminds us that God is *'my fortress, my refuge in times of trouble. O my Strength, I sing praise to you; you, O God, are my fortress, my loving God.'* Psalm 59:16b, 17

# PRAYER

Lord, I do not know why I am here in this awful situation, but I know that it is affecting all of the family. Give me strength and courage to face this head on, so that those I love may be able to come along side me and not fear that they will further upset me. Help us to realise that we are in this together and we need your strength and love to overcome our fear and uncertainty. Give us a rock-sure realisation that you are our fortress and strength and put a song of praise in my heart and mouth, in your precious name, my Lord and Redeemer. Amen.

# GOD CARES FOR HIS CREATURES

## STARRY, STARRY NIGHT

*He heals the broken-hearted, and binds up their wounds. He determines the number of the stars; he gives to all of them their names. Great is our Lord, and abundant in power; his understanding is beyond measure.*
  Psalm 147:3-5 (NRSV)

Vincent van Gogh wrote to his brother Theo, "This morning I saw the country from my window a long time before sunrise, with nothing but the morning star, which looked very big." It was his inspiration to paint the picture known as 'The Starry Night'. This led Don McLean to write the words of the lyric 'Starry, Starry Night', which became a number one hit in the UK. When I read this I wondered how often do the things we see have such an impression on us that they inspire us to creative thought or action, or do we simply look but not assimilate.

Where we live is far from neighbours and towns, so there is no light pollution. It's beautiful to go out on a crisp cloudless night for a walk with the dogs. It's then that you can see the Milky Way and identify the constellations. We live in such an amazing universe that this never ceases to draw my thoughts and problems into perspective. As a child I used to look out at the night sky and watch for 'shooting stars' because I thought that when you saw one you could have a wish which would come true. I'm older now, and know that 'shooting stars' are not stars at all, but small meteoroids burning up as they enter the earth's upper atmosphere. However it's still an awesome sight which expands my thoughts. My encyclopedia tells me that there are probably more than one hundred and seventy billion galaxies in the observable universe. How my mind struggles with one billion as a number, let alone more than one hundred and seventy billion. I just know that there is no end to the number of stars that I can see, and as far as distance goes, it is unimaginable. I want to sing, "How great is our God". The Psalmist tells us that, *"He determines the number of the stars; he gives to all of them their names."* Psalm 147:4. He also tells us that, *"He heals the broken-hearted, and binds up their wounds."* (v3) Your mood may be broken-hearted at the moment, and feelings of isolation may envelop you, but God's understanding is beyond measure, and his love for you is everlasting. He will never leave you nor forsake you.

## PRAYER

Dear God, you seem distant and remote at times, especially when I feel isolated and alone. Thank you that your word says that you are understanding beyond measure, and that your power is abundant. I need that assurance now, and I need you to bind up my wounds, and touch me with your healing love. I am such a tiny part of this great universe that you have created, but as you have named each of the billions of stars, I know that you know me by name. I am comforted by this, and praise your holy Name, through Jesus Christ our Lord. Amen.

# MESSING ABOUT IN BOATS

There's nothing quite like messing about in boats. How right Mr Toad of Toad Hall is, in the book, 'Wind in the Willows'; and holidays are just the time for it. A couple of weeks ago we took a Monday off to go sailing. We had planned it for some time and hoped the weather would be good, and it was, but not for sailing, for there was hardly a breath of wind. Nevertheless the sandwiches were made, and the sun was splitting the sky, so we raised sail and slipped our mooring. With the Quoile basin behind us and no plan other than avoiding pladdies, those submerged and part submerged islands in Strangford Lough, we started to take notice of our surroundings. The water was crystal clear, and you could see down to quite a depth. First we saw one or two jelly fish, and then shoals of them in all shapes and sizes, and they just kept coming... clear ones with beautiful lilac circles, white ones, brown ones with long frond-like tentacles and the occasional huge Portuguese man-of-war. How attractive they looked with their umbrella shape contracting and expanding as they swam gently along, and my mind was drawn to words in the Book Ecclesiasticus (Aporcypha): *By his plan he stilled the deep and planted islands in it. Those who sail the sea tell of its dangers, and we marvel at what we hear. In it are strange and marvellous creatures, all kinds of living things, and huge sea-monsters.* Ecclesiasticus 43:23-25

*Where can we find the strength to praise him? For he is greater than all his works. Awesome is the Lord and very great, and marvellous is his power.* (43:28-29)

When we take the opportunity to put aside the things that are happening in life and grasp the chance of some time outdoors, God draws our thoughts to the wonders of creation. There we begin to understand God's power and majesty, but also his care for all his creatures, great and small. None are insignificant.

## A PRAYER FOR TODAY

Loving Heavenly Father, your creation tells of your glory and love. Through the reminders of you around me, draw me to yourself, and still my anxious thoughts and worries. Fill me with your peace and love and encircle me with your Spirit, so that I may feel safe, for I ask in Jesus' name. Amen.

# BOTTLE IT?

*Record my lament; list my tears on your scroll -- are they not in your record?* Psalm 56:8

Do you read the newspaper? Perhaps you just go on-line and pick up the headlines, or maybe you really read every article word for word, because you want to know the news thoroughly; you want to keep up with events in the world. Sometimes what we read really impacts us. It can even cause us distress when we think about what other people have to deal with. We wonder how they could have landed in their situation, but we realise that at times things just happen. We also wonder how they can cope; who is there to help them and what the outcome will be. We do not like to put ourselves in other people's shoes when they are in trouble. However when you think of it, you can never really put yourself in another's shoes. Each person has to deal with their own difficulties. You only realise that when you are in a troublesome situation yourself. But it is knowing that you are not really alone that helps, because God has promised that he will never leave you or forsake you,

The Psalmist reminds us that even our very tears are listed in God's record, because he cares that much. The King James Version of the Bible translates Psalm 56:8 as: *Thou tellest my wanderings: put thou my tears into thy bottle: are they not in thy book?* Our very tears are noted by God. That may amaze us, because people round us so often say: 'Don't cry!' They cannot bear our sadness. God holds us during our troubled times, noting each very tear. We can be absolutely honest with him and we do not have to hide anything from him. The good news is that nothing is ever wasted. God can use your experience to help others, if you are willing to be open to him and let him use you.

## A PRAYER FOR TODAY

Loving Lord, thank you that you care for me so much that even my tears are important to you. Thank you that you miss none of them. I do not want to upset my family so I try to hide my tears from them. It makes me feel alone in this, and I need to see you. I need to be able to read you in events. I need to hear you. Strengthen my sight, and let me see the true meaning of events, so that I may know that it is you when you give me a sign; so that I may hear when you invite me to do something that will help someone else. Thank you that you understand my sadness.

Amen.

## THE GOD WHO CARES

According to Greek mythology, Sisyphus was once a cruel king of Corinth. When he died, he was eternally condemned to push a giant boulder up a steep hill. The closer he got to the top of the hill, the steeper the hill became. Every time, just as he was about to reach the top of the hill, he lost control of the boulder, it rolled over him and back to the bottom of the hill where Sisyphus had to start again.

Life can feel like that sometimes, can't it? Just when you are recovering from one problem, along comes something else to send you hurtling back to the bottom of the hill.

I wonder can you remember what happened when, as a child, you fell and hurt yourself? To whom did you run? When I was growing up in Downpatrick, there was nothing I liked better than to run up the Cathedral hill with my tricycle, jump on and fly down the other side. One time though, my school girdle got caught in the chain and off I flew head first landing in a sorry heap in the middle of the road. From nowhere, a stranger appeared. He disentangled my girdle from the trike and I went running to find my mother, without even thanking the man for having come to my rescue. When children hurt themselves, they quite naturally run to the person who loves them most because they know that that person will do all in their power to take away the pain that they are suffering.

So who do grown ups run to when they are suffering, when

illness or tragedy knocks on their door? Unfortunately, some people let their problems push them away from God. They become bitter and begin to question God's love, which takes them further and further away from God.

If we are going to face our troubles, our illnesses head on, we must allow them to push us closer to God. The real answers to life's problems are not to be found in magazine columns or television talk shows. The real answers to life's problems are to be found in the Word of God. There is no problem that God cannot solve. He loves us more than we could ever love ourselves and he understands us better than we could ever understand ourselves. He knows what we need and when we need it and why we need it

Life is not a sprint, it is more like a marathon with many twists and turns and diversions. When Paul came to the end of his life, he was able to say, *'I have fought a good fight, I have finished my course, I have kept the faith.'* 2 Timothy 4:7

We must always allow our illness, our troubles, to push us to God. Like a child who is in pain runs to a loving parent for their healing touch, we must run to God for his healing touch. God does not always offer an easy cure. He does not always offer a way out. Sometimes he offers a way through. He offers the grace to bear the sickness for his glory.

When Jesus sent out his disciples it was with a sense of urgency to bring about healing of soul and body alike. The harvest is still plentiful and the need for willing workers remains. We must never doubt that God is still sending his servants out to suffering people everywhere. When Jesus commissioned the disciples and sent them out it was not a suggestion that they *'Heal the sick, raise the dead, cleanse those who have leprosy, drive out demons. Freely you have*

144

received, freely give.' Matthew 10:5-8  On the contrary, it was an instruction, a command and he is still commanding his followers today to do the same. If we ever doubt our Lord's promises, then let us remember Job. In spite of all his troubles and even the rejection of his wife and friends, Job hung in there with God. Job believed in the promises of God, his troubles and afflictions pushed him towards God not away from him. He knew that he could trust in God to bring him through his troubles.

## A PRAYER

We give you thanks, O God, for your healing ministry. We thank you that you not only care for the health of our spirit, but for our minds and bodies as well. Help us always to call upon you and your church for all our healing needs. For Christ's sake. Amen.

# IF YOU CAN'T STAND THE HEAT!

*'Then Nebuchadnezzar was furious with Shadrach, Mesach and Abednego, and his attitude towards them changed. He ordered the furnace to be heated seven times hotter than usual, and commanded some of the strongest soldiers in his army to tie up Shadrach, Mesach and Abednego and throw them into the blazing furnace.'*
Daniel 3: 19–20

The book of Daniel opens with the invasion of Judah by the Babylonians. Many young Israelites were captured and taken to Babylon. Among those taken prisoner were our three friends Shadrach, Mesach and Abednego along with their friend Daniel. Daniel is not a long book and is well worth the read.

Nebuchannezzar was furious to hear that our three friends refused to worship the Babylonian gods or bow down to worship their images of gold. And so, along came the fiery furnace as punishment. But God had other plans and rescued the young men from the flames.

If God could deliver these young men from a fiery furnace, it should naturally follow that he can deliver us from whatever kind of trouble we are in. He IS still in control of this world. Satan can do his worst, but God is and always will be in control. The sooner we accept that God has the final authority over everything, the better off we will be. As believers, we know that God is working all things together for our good (Romans 8:28). While God is not the source of our troubles, He can use those troubles and overrule them to produce positive results in our lives. This means that no matter what problems or difficulties we face in our path of life, God CAN use them for good. He may use our problems and difficulties to teach us great lessons and to bring us to a point of repentance. It is only when we realise and accept the sovereign rule of God over everything that we can place our complete trust in him. Trusting God completely doesn't mean that he has to meet our needs in a way that we have already decided. God knows best and his time is best.

As God works in our lives, He very often shows us His will and purposes in the very circumstances in which we are struggling. I'm sure you will agree that there are many, many times in our lives when we try to tell God how to solve our problems. We want to make absolutely sure, beyond a shadow of doubt that God is not going to throw us into the proverbial "fiery furnace". We want to be assured that God will save and deliver us BEFORE we face any trouble.

Time and time again, the Bible tells us that God will deliver us IN our troubles rather than FROM our troubles. Paul says in 2 Corinthians 1: 4 that God is the God who *comforts us in all our troubles, so that we can comfort those in any trouble with the comfort we ourselves have received from God.* God allowed these young men to stay in the fiery furnace just long enough for them to realise the greatness of His deliverance and he allowed them to stay in the fiery furnace long enough for the Babylonians to realize the same.

It is never fun going through the furnace of illness or suffering or watching a loved one go through it, but when you do, you can be sure that God is with you. Suffering tends to flatten our pride and self-dependence and draws us closer to God. Isn't it better to be in a fiery furnace WITH Christ than in a place of luxury and opulence without him?

# PRAYER

God my Father, in my distress, in my pain, in this illness, I feel so far away from you.   Which one of us has moved?

# TINY THINGS

It was a beautiful day, so we went sailing on Strangford Lough. The sun was shining and there was enough wind to move us along at a good pace. We left the mooring in the Quoile Basin and headed towards Killyleagh. The Mourne Mountains were outlined behind us and the beauty of God's creation was evident all around. Although we were moving with wind and tide, there was a sense of timelessness. It gave an opportunity to put everyday things into perspective; and allow the clamouring problems of work to recede.

But it was over too soon, a brief moment in a hectic timetable, a day for refreshment and time to think. When we came to lift our mooring, I noticed a spider at the bow, painstakingly spinning its web. How did it get there, for the mooring had to be reached by small dingy? Such a tiny thing, it would have been easy to miss.

There are many times in life that we are passed by, at work or even at home, times when we have been hurt and wonder if we matter at all.

Remember that God loves you. He loves you even though He knows you better than anyone else does. Jesus' words tell us that. They are recorded for us in Luke 12:7

*Are not five sparrows sold for two pennies? Yet not one of them is forgotten by God. Indeed the very hairs on your head are numbered.*

No matter how insignificant we feel, we are not forgotten by God, even the very hairs on our head are numbered.

# A PRAYER FOR TODAY

Dear Heavenly Father, you seem very close on the good days, when the sun shines, and I feel that I can cope. Help me to remember that you are always with me, at all times of my life: on good days and on bad days; and remind me that you care for me and my life in the tiniest of detail. I ask through Jesus Christ our Lord. Amen.

# THE BEAUTY OF GOD'S CREATION

## HONEYCOMB

Pure honey on hot toast, the sheer luxury of it! As I stretched out my hand for the honey in the honey comb I marvelled at the amazing engineering of the comb. There it was - row upon row of six sided rooms with walls of wax. What incredible architects bees are, for each room was the same size with each of the three pairs of walls facing the other. How on earth does the bee know that the hexagon has the smallest circumference, therefore requiring the smallest amount of building material?

How do they know that the hexagon cells are the best and most economical plan? Who told them? Yet they do it without blueprints or drawing boards or protractors; and every cell is perfect – just the size to fit a bee. More than that, when bees fly off to the fields looking for nectar and pollen they may have to travel several miles, searching in several directions, yet they fly straight back to the hive. Who told them how to do it? What sort of navigational equipment do they possess? And how do they communicate to the others the location of the treasure they have found, for immediately other bees will leave the hive and go directly to the source?

Glory to God for such wonders! It seems the most natural thing to exclaim because of the many examples in nature of animals acting as if they 'knew', and thus giving witness to the infinite intelligence of their Creator.

The writer of Chronicles says:

*O give thanks to the LORD, sing praises to him, tell of all his wonderful works.* 1 Chron 16:9

## A PRAYER FOR TODAY

Dear God, your majesty and wonder are over all the earth, yet your presence is felt in the detail, even in the smallest feature. When I look at the marvels of your creation I know that you comprehend the cells and tissues in my body, their workings and their disease. Refresh and renew me in the minuteness of my being; body, mind and spirit, and give all who have care of me, your wisdom and understanding, through Jesus Christ our Lord. Amen.

# FLOWER POWER

*'Consider how the lilies grow. They do not labour or spin. Yet, I tell you, not even Solomon in all his splendour was dressed like one of these. If that is how God clothes the grass of the field, which is here today, and tomorrow is thrown into the fire, how much more will he clothe you, O you of little faith!'*

Luke 12:27-28

'What do you see?' the Master asked, as the students gathered round.
'I see lilium chalcedonicum, I think,' said Thomas, with a frown.
And all the students were puzzled too, for neither were we sure of the answer that the Master sought
in the field of red and green and blue.

'What do you see?' he asked again, and our Matthew, counting slowly said,
'Three scarlet petals and four leaves of green – but I cannot count them all.
And all together we nodded as we looked around that day,
For thousands upon thousands of the blooms were on display.

'What do you see?' the Master pressed, and Judas spoke out next.
'A fallow field which, ploughed and sown, could a goodly profit yield.'
And we marvelled at our fellow who could see gain in every place,
But there, that day, material wealth seemed strangely out of place.

'What do you see?' The Master's challenge had still not been met.

'A symbol of our freedom. The emblem of our land!'

And we, the students, looked confused at the sword in Simon's hand,

Embarrassed by our Zealot's image of struggle for freedom in an occupied land.

Then Mary rose and picked a bloom – a stillness filled the crowd -

'I love you, Master,' was all she said, and laid the flower down as a tribute to her gentle Lord.

Then, with the love gift at his feet, she asked the only question left.

'What should we see?' our Mary asked, and we all leaned close to hear.

'A caring God,' our Master said, 'who clothes the common flower with beauty,

excelling that of kings, and cares for all his world – here and in every place,

and of all the wonders he has made, you, yes you, are the objects of his grace.'

And then our eyes were opened, and we saw the field anew,

Beyond the leaves, beyond the colours, our Creator stood on view,

And never again did we see the world through the limits of physical sight,

For the Master had helped us to see deeper, helped us to see further, helped us to see aright –

Helped us to see the God who lies behind every field, every flower, every face.

*Adapted from 'Rivers in the Desert' Edited by Rowland Croucher 1991 'Consider how the lilies grow.'*

# GLORIOUS TECHNICOLOUR

Summer mornings are wonderful. You wake early and open your eyes to the reality of light, colour, motion and perspective… There's more to vision than meets the eye, for when we open our eyes we translate a mass of information into images that make sense. We see with our eyes, and what we see helps us to believe. Seeing is believing! Imagine your living room with the sofa and chairs in position, the cupboards, the TV, the DVD player all there. Imagine the position of the ornaments and the pictures on the wall. Everything is in its place. Now try to imagine the same scene with the lights turned off. Everything is still in its place, but that may be difficult to believe, if you believe only what you can see. Without light we cannot see to believe. The psalmist wrote: *The LORD is my light and my salvation.* Psalm 27:1a

For too many people religion seems to take the entire colour out of life, limiting them in their activities, but there's more to God's light than that. In His light a wonderful world of colour opens up before our eyes. Jesus promised his followers: *I came that you may have life and have it abundantly.* John 10:10 Abundant life is what God, the true light, is all about. Today, just take a minute or two to look around you at our world filled with colour, the fields, the trees, the sky, the sea, and the myriad array of flowers of every hue, and praise God for his goodness.

*I will sing of your steadfast love, O LORD, forever; with my mouth I will proclaim your faithfulness to all generations.*
Psalm 89:1

## A PRAYER FOR TODAY

Dear Lord, give me a heart of praise that I may sing of your goodness, in times of health and prosperity and in times of disease and financial stringency. Open my mind to the glory of your goodness and your rainbow of hope. I ask in Jesus' name. Amen.

# COMMON! I THINK NOT!

*"What are human beings that you are mindful of them, or mortals, that you care for them? You have made them for a little while lower than the angels; you have crowned them with glory and honour, subjecting all things under their feet."* Hebrews 26b-8a (NRSV)

Walking the dogs down the lane and over the causeway to our home one day I was amazed by a flash of shimmering blue or was it green? The burst of colour exploded on my mind and I searched with my eyes to see where it had gone. The dogs, normally so vigilant, were quite oblivious to this iridescent explosion of colour into my view, and its equally sudden departure. Could I have imagined it? Certainly not! It was real, not imaginary, and I simply knew what it had been. It was a kingfisher, with its unmistakable bright greenish blue and orange plumage. They say that they are birds of slow moving or still water, yet they themselves move with such speed, that it is unusual to see them. Often all that you see is the flash of shimmering malachite plumage. Why therefore does the bird book call them the 'Common Kingfisher', because 'common' is not what we experience in the northern parts of these isles. They are such shy birds, but so very beautiful. It isn't the pigment of their feathers that causes their wonderful colours, but it is the structure of the feathers, which causes scattering of blue light. This experience of light and colour left me excited and in wonder of nature. I better understood the words, 'Glorious Technicolour' I used to see at the cinema on the movie credits. How I longed to see him again, yet I knew just how fortunate I had been to see him at all.

A friend who was visiting for a few days also had the excitement of seeing this magnificent bird. She said, "I know why they call him 'king'. It is because he points our thoughts to the Creator, the King of all the earth." I couldn't agree with her more. There is so much in nature which points us to God and reminds us of his care for his world. How, then can we doubt that he has care of us, whom he made a little lower than the angels, when we so clearly see his care for his birds of the air. The writer of the Letter to the Hebrews asks: *"What are human beings that you are mindful of them, or mortals, that you care for them?"* Then he answers his own question with words to encourage and hold us: *"You have made them for a little while lower than the angels."*

## PRAYER

Heavenly Father, thank you for the signs of your goodness and care that I see in the world all around me. Keep me under the shadow of your wing and protect me when I am feeling down, especially at the moment when things are difficult to come to terms with and work through. Help me to hold onto you during this time knowing that you care for me, and help me to look to tomorrow with renewed hope and expectation. Encourage me into a positive attitude and let me show my gratitude, not just to you, but to all who are treating me and helping me get better, through Jesus Christ our Lord. Amen.

# PRAYER

## DOES PRAYER WORK?

*"When you pray, go into your room, close the door and pray to your Father, who is unseen. Then your Father, who sees what is done in secret, will reward you."* Matthew 6:6

There was once a priest in Dublin who parked his car on a rather steep hill close to his church. His little terrier dog was lying on the back seat out of sight of any passers-by. The priest got out of the car and turned to lock the doors with his usual parting command to the dog. *"Stay!"* he ordered loudly, to an apparently empty car. *"Stay!"* An elderly gentleman was watching the performance with amused interest. Grinning, he said, *"Reverend, I admire your faith, but why don't you just try putting on the handbrake?"*

To the mind of the unbeliever, watching someone praying is like watching someone say, *"Stay"*, to their car, fully expecting it to obey. To the unbeliever, prayer is an exercise in futility and, even we, at times, can be guilty of accusing God of not hearing our prayers, or hearing them but not answering them.

Jesus believed in prayer. He was constantly to be found in communication with God and maybe that is why his disciples asked him to teach them to pray.

*"This, then, is how you should pray:*
*" ' Our Father in heaven......' "* Matthew 6: 9-13

I believe that perhaps the most important element in prayer may be the act of praying itself. Prayer acknowledges our dependence on God. It acknowledges God's power and majesty and our own inadequacy and need. So what if we say the same thing every time we pray? The important thing is that we are daily spending time with God.

Sometimes, particularly when we are ill, it is very difficult to pray, especially if we blame God for our sickness and are angry with him for "doing this" to us; but make no mistake, illness is not, and never will be, from God, but he is with us in all the pains we suffer. When it is hardest to pray, we should pray the hardest!

We can trust God. The answer to our prayers may not be just the answer we had prescribed, but God can be trusted. Our prayers will not go unheeded. May we always count it a blessing when God delays the answer to our prayers in order to enlarge our capacity to receive.

*"Our Father in heaven, hallowed be your name, your kingdom come, your will be done on earth as in heaven. Give us today our daily bread. Forgive us our sins, as we forgive those who sin against us. Lead us not into temptation, but deliver us from evil. For the kingdom the power and the glory are yours now and for ever." AMEN.*

# PRAYERS FOR YOUR USE

We have found that the times that it is most difficult to pray are when you are in real difficulty, or have what appears to be insurmountable problems, particularly those concerning your health and even existence. These circumstances are the very times that you should pray, but the words refuse to come. We have therefore included some prayers for your use, which may see you through the time of immobility, and set you free to make your own requests and responses to our Father God.

## I CANNOT PRAY FOR MYSELF

Dear Lord,
I have come to a time when I cannot pray for myself,
and I have to leave it to others.
All I can think of is the treatment,
and the appointments that I have to keep.
My thoughts are all about keeping alive and surviving this day.
I know that there is no point in grumbling
as it wears my family and friends out,
and I am afraid, and afraid of being on my own.
I don't want to be isolated.
Complaining will not make me healthy.
I will have to get used to it.
I know that St Paul says that
the Spirit himself intercedes for us when we are weak.
I am at a time that I do not know what I should pray for.
I know that everyone round me is working hard

161

to make an unbearable situation bearable,
and many are praying for me.
Maybe, Lord, you could bless them for the help they are giving
me. I do not know how to do it myself.
Hold me during this difficult time,
and carry me through these troubles.
Amen.


## TEST RESULT DAY

O Lord,
let me be conscious of your real presence
even when my sky is covered with clouds,
and things round about me feel gloomy and apprehensive.
I have to face the doctor
and listen to the results of the tests that were taken.
Give me all the courage that I need
and help me to know that you are there in the midst of this.
Lord, even now you know the outcome,
so I ask that you wrap your loving arms around me
and strengthen me,
and give me an eternal perspective
beyond my present trouble,
for I ask in Jesus' precious name.
Amen.

## IN THE WHIRLWIND

Dear Lord,
there is so much going on at the moment
and all appointments follow rapidly one upon another,
so that I do not seem as if I have time to catch my breath.
It is as though everything is shouting to be done at once, that
I cannot hear myself think,
let alone hear your voice.
Lord, I am holding onto my faith through this whirlwind,
in the hope that I will hear your voice again,
calming me into a silence,
and restoring my soul to peace.
Speak to me to reassure me,
even a little whisper.
Thank you.
Amen.

The LORD said (to Elijah), "Go out and stand on the mountain in the presence of the LORD, for the LORD is about to pass by."

Then a great and powerful wind tore the mountains apart and shattered the rocks before the LORD, but the LORD was not in the wind.

*After the wind there was an earthquake, but the LORD was not in the earthquake. After the earthquake came a fire, but the LORD was not in the fire. And after the fire came a gentle whisper.* 1 Kings 19:11-12 (NIV)

DEAR Lord and Father of mankind,
forgive our foolish ways;
re-clothe us in our rightful mind,
in purer lives thy service find,
in deeper reverence, praise.

2  In simple trust like theirs who heard,
beside the Syrian sea,
the gracious calling of the Lord,
let us like them, without a word
rise up and follow thee.

3  O Sabbath rest by Galilee,
O calm of hills above,
where Jesus knelt to share with thee
the silence of eternity,
interpreted by love.

4  Drop thy still dews of quietness,
till all our strivings cease;
take from our souls the strain and stress,
and let our ordered lives confess
the beauty of thy peace.

5  Breathe through the heats of our desire
thy coolness and thy balm;
let sense be dumb, let flesh retire;
speak through the earthquake, wind and fire,
O still small voice of calm.

John G Whittier (1807-92)

## 'I WILL BE WITH YOU'

Lord, this cannot be.
I cannot have cancer.
That happens to other people.
I find it so hard to take in.
Thank you for the doctor who reassured me
that although I am stunned it is not a death sentence,
there are thousands of survivors,
and that means that there is always hope.
I know that I can trust you,
even with this dreadful diagnosis,
and that you will never leave me.
You have promised not to leave me or forsake me.
I feel fear rising in me,
but I am reminding myself that you are very close
and that excites me.
Can this be the start of an exciting journey together?
You may have to carry me on the way,
but that will keep me close to you.
I am grateful for that.
Thank you for your promises which hold me.
Amen.


Isaiah 43:2
*When you pass through the waters, I will be with you; and when
you pass through the rivers, they will not sweep over you. (NIV)*

Church Hymnal 383  Tune: *Quam dilecta*

Lord, be thy word my rule;
in it may I rejoice:
thy glory be my aim,
thy holy will my choice;

thy promises my hope;
thy providence my guard;
thine arm my strong support;
thyself my great reward.
      *Christopher Wordsworth (1807-85)*


## WHEN YOU ARE SCARED

Lord, I am scared.
The thought of what I'm facing makes my heart almost stop.
Help me to hand all my worries over to you
for you are the helper of the helpless.
My tank is running on empty!
I desperately need your help!
Amen.

## WHEN YOU FEEL DOWN

Lord, I feel so alone.  You seem a million miles away.
I am worn out and everything has got on top of me.
Didn't you say somewhere that you would never leave me,
that you would be with me to the close of the age?
Lord, I need to feel your presence now!
Amen.


## IS GOD THERE?

God, are you really there?  I'm not sure any more.  My faith is
wavering, it's as thin as gossamer.
God, I do believe, please help my unbelief.
Amen.


## ILLNESS

Lord, I am devastated by this illness
and the suddenness with which it came upon me.
Help me to be patient as I look to you for healing and wholeness.
In Jesus' name.
Amen.

## SEARCHING FOR PEACE

Heavenly Father, I feel as if I am on a storm-tossed boat
in the middle of a raging, angry sea.  I am troubled and upset.
Come alongside me with your comfort and peace,
strength and encouragement.
Quieten my feelings,
calm my troubled spirit.
Speak to me of your peace, that peace that the world
cannot give.
Abba Father, speak those words to me,
"Peace, be still!"
Amen.


## A SHORT PRAYER

Lord, help me to remember
That nothing is going to happen to me today
That You and I together can't handle.


## THE JESUS PRAYER

Lord Jesus Christ,
Son of God,
Have mercy on me, a sinner.

## ST. IGNATIUS OF LOYOLA' PRAYER
## AGAINST DEPRESSION

O Christ Jesus
When all is darkness
And we feel our weakness and helplessness,
Give us the sense of Your presence,
Your love and your strength.
Help us to have perfect trust
In your protecting love
And strengthening power,
So that nothing may frighten or worry us,
For, living close to you,
We shall see Your hand,
Your purpose, Your will through all things.
Amen


## ENCOURAGEMENT

Let nothing disturb you
Let nothing frighten you,
All things are passing away:
God never changes.
Patience obtains all things
Whoever has God lacks nothing;
God alone suffices.
St. Teresa of Avila

## GOING INTO HOSPITAL

Lord Jesus,
stay close to me as I go into hospital.
May I experience your presence and healing
among the medical staff.
Guard my heart from anxiety
and strengthen me in the gift of faith,
so that my hope rests solely in you.
Through your grace prepare me for
the daily routine of the ward,
and help me to be a symbol of your love
to those around me.
In Jesus' name. Amen.


## FOR SLEEP

Grant me a quiet night,
O Lord, and give me rest,
For I am tired and need sleep.
Watch over me with your love
in the silence of the night,
and let me rest in you
like a child in its mother's arms.
I place my trust in you,
My God.
Amen.

## BEFORE AN OPERATION

Almighty God,
You know my inmost being,
the secrets of my body and soul.
Fill my heart with trust, even as I fear.
Bless the surgeons and nurses
and all who work to help me
with gifts of healing and care.
Be near to me,
gently sustaining me,
and supporting them in their skills.
Amen.


## PRAYER BEFORE FIRST CHEMOTHERAPY

Dear loving Father, I hardly know what to pray for today. This is all a big unknown for me, and I need to feel your strengthening presence with me as I enter this strange, new world of chemotherapy. Please help me to keep positive, in the knowledge that this treatment is being offered to blast the cancer away. Bless the highly specialised medical staff who will prescribe and administer the drugs, and give me courage to face needles and drips with quiet assurance. Help me to feel you near me like never before, even in the hands of the nurses, as they carry out your work of healing in me. In Jesus' name. Amen.

## PRAYER FOLLOWING FIRST CHEMOTHERAPY

Lord God, I have come through the first session safely, and I want to thank you for being with me. Now I have only __ more to go. You know how tired I am now: please give me good, healing rest and sleep, that I may feel better tomorrow. I ask that I may not suffer too much from any side-effects, but if this should happen, then I pray that the doctors will be able to lessen it's unpleasantness. Please help this dose to do its work of ridding my body of the cancerous cells, and restoring me to health. In Jesus' name. Amen.

Loving Father,
I put myself into your hands.
Deliver me from fear of pain and the unknown.
Guide the surgeon, the anesthetist
and the theatre staff by your Spirit.
Anoint them as servants of your healing power,
and while I am unconscious
may my deepest thoughts and feelings rest in you.
May I sleep in your peace,
and awake to praise your mercy and goodness.
In the name of Jesus.
Amen.

## PRAYERS FOR HEALING

Dear Lord Jesus
you know the depths of my need in body, mind and spirit.
I surrender myself to you in faith,
asking you to touch me with your healing hand, so that:
in body my health and strength will be renewed,
in mind I will know your peace,
in spirit I will be set free from worry and anxiety.
I ask this in your name and for your sake.
Amen.

Seagoe Parish Healing Prayer Group


Lord Jesus Christ, touch me with your healing,
encircle me in your love
and enfold me in your peace;
so that I may live this day in quietness of mind
and tranquillity of spirit,
and may your name
be glorified above all for ever.
Amen.

The Church's Ministry of Healing: The Mount

## GREAT IS THY FAITHFULNESS

Dear Lord,
things are tough and I am weary.
I have no energy for the fight,
which seems endless.
Somewhere in my mind the words,
'Strength for the day and bright hope for tomorrow,'
are running round.
I cannot remember where they come from,
but that is exactly what I need.
Please give me just enough strength for this day,
and a new hope to sustain me,
so that I can move forward into tomorrow
with renewed confidence.
I am fearful of this new treatment I have to undergo,
so I am looking to you to bring me through it.
Help me to feel your presence with me during it all.
Thank you.
Amen.

Great is thy faithfulness, O God my Father,
there is no shadow of turning with thee;
thou changest not, thy compassions, they fail not,
as thou hast been thou for ever wilt be.

*Great is thy faithfulness, great is thy faithfulness,*
*morning by morning new mercies I see;*
*all I have needed thy hand hath provided,*
*great is thy faithfulness, Lord, unto me!*

Summer and winter, and spring-time and harvest,
sun, moon and stars in their courses above,
join with all nature in manifold witness
to thy great faithfulness, mercy and love.

Pardon for sin and a peace that endureth,
thine own dear presence to cheer and to guide;
strength for today and bright hope for tomorrow,
blessings all mine, and ten thousand beside!

Thomas Chisholm (1866-1960)
Based on Lamentations 3:22-23; Genesis 8:22.

## THANKSGIVING

Thanks be to thee,
my Lord Jesus Christ,
For all the benefits which thou hast given me,
For all the pains and insults which thou hast bourn for me.
O most merciful Redeemer, Friend and Brother,
May I know thee more clearly,
Love thee more dearly,
And follow thee more nearly.
Amen.
*Richard of Chichester*